BICYCLE THIEVES

BICYCLE THIEVES

a film by

Vittorio De Sica

translated by Simon Hartog

faber and faber
LONDON · BOSTON

First published in 1968 by Lorrimer Publishing Limited
First published in 1994 by
Faber and Faber Limited
3 Queen Square London WC1N 3AU
Printed in England by Clays Ltd, St Ives plc

English translation © Lorrimer Publishing Limited, 1968

Original Italian language film entitled *Ladri di Biciclette*
© PDS (Producaioni De Sica), 1948
Original French language edition entitled
Le Voleur de Bicyclette © l'Avant-Scène due Cinema, 1967

Introduction © Simon Hartog, 1968

Stills courtesy of l'Avant-Scène du Cinéma and the
British Film Institute

A CIP record for this book is available
from the British Library

ISBN 0–571–12561–1

2 4 6 8 10 9 7 5 3 1

CONTENTS

INTRODUCTION

' I spent months without finding a
backer for *Bicycle Thieves*. Then
one day, an American producer
offered me millions. There was
only one condition. Cary Grant
had to play the part of the worker.
I refused . . .'

Vittorio De Sica from *Le Monde*,
March 4th, 1955.

The knowing smile provoked by this footnote to film history
betrays the unequivocal imprint, clear even in its defects,
which *Bicycle Thieves* has made on the cinema's perception
of its own power and potentiality. *Bicycle Thieves* is one of
those few frozen moments in film history when everything
flies together, where everything fits. These exceptional
moments are of their nature fragile and fleeting. The film,
which concentrates the essence of an epoch, is like the single
flash of lightning which illuminates the pitch black night ever
so briefly. The landscape is seldom so easily discernible.

At a time when that curious beast, Occidental Man, had
yet again to rationalise the havoc he had wrought, this film
struck a simple chord which found sympathetic echoes in minds
which needed hope. Its fame and impact were enshrined in
critical adulation and Vatican disapproval. In the late fifties,
at one of those obscene spectacles in which film critics and
historians are wont to take part, *Bicycle Thieves* was pro-
claimed one of the ten best films ever made. Today, the

6

jaundiced eye bears the tale less well. It still retains the essence of the movement in which it took such exemplar part. It is the heart, if not the mind of neo-realism, a metaphor which also serves to distinguish its director and its script writer. But, except for those who still insist on equating its goodness of intention with its value as a film — a decadent distinction which only the time and land in which we live permits — *Bicycle Thieves* contains within itself the seeds of its own mummification.

The film is born of a theory which is not a theory but a style — a style which changes the wallpaper without challenging the principles inherent in the structure. In the end it is these principles which render the stylistic redecoration futile. In defence of his stylistic terms of reference De Sica rejected Cary Grant's participation, but he did this without rejecting the structural assumptions in the script which permitted Cary Grant to even be considered for the part. In *Bicycle Thieves* the medium molests the message. Its memorable aesthetic is not sufficiently total to support its revolutionary tunic.

This film, or any neo-realist film worthy of the name, creates the recurring response, ' Oh, how true to life! ' And it is, as much as any artefact can be. Neo-realism demands photographic verisimilitude in each frame of the film, a mirror image, a snap ' taken from life '. The setting, the location, is, of course, also of crucial importance — some locations being more realistic than others. These are the visual limits of neo-realism. André Bazin, one of the ablest witnesses for the defence, unintentionally defines the gulf : '. . . *Bicycle Thieves* is one of the first examples of pure cinema. No more actors, no more plot, no more mise-en-scène. It is in the end the perfect aesthetic illusion of reality : no more cinema.'[1] The cinema becomes life — within the static frame. As soon as the picture moves, the validity of the style is questioned, and

[1] p. 59, André Bazin, *Qu'est-ce que le cinéma?* IV. Une esthétique de la réalité : le néo-réalisme, Les Editions du Cerf, Paris, 1962.

when the cut — however unobtrusive — comes, the film's construction subjugates its style. The illusion of reality disappears. De Sica's refusal to use Cary Grant should not obscure the fact that the film has a hero who wanders through one of the most exquisitely constructed, subtly controlled, and geographically conscious scripts ever filmed. Every new scene, each new line at once clarifies Antonio Ricci's social situation and closes the trap in which he is caught even tighter. Ricci, like the lone Western hero, or the tough detective, is searching for justice. Like them, he is isolated, cut off from society, involved in a nightmare chase. Unlike them, he is not faced by evil individuals but an evil system which is manifest in individual indifference. He, like them, attracts our sympathy because we know he has been wronged and because, when he is not demonstrating his humanity, he is outnumbered. With its traditional musical comment and its sympathy demanding devices, its individual hero and his counter-pointing son[2], the construction and conception of *Bicycle Thieves* are not threatened by the stylistic adjustments of using ' real ' people and ' authentic ' sets. Perhaps in the end though, it was precisely this failure of neo-realism which dealt Hollywood its definitive ace of spades.

The great appeal of neo-realism is due in some ways to the partial nature of its aesthetic attack. It is ' realistic ' without being ' real ', and the same is true of its political commitment. The populist concern for daily life catapults the two line news item of a bicycle theft into tragedy. A man without his bike cannot work. He is, as a result, isolated from institutions and alternatives. It is an individual and external tragedy from which it is not easy to generalise. Not only because it is tendentious and easily resolved but also because the miniaturisation of a social inadequacy permits the moral response to the situation to degenerate into an easily digestible fatalism. The choral revolutionary film is not only tactically more adequate

---

[2] The musical metaphor which so accurately describes Bruno's function in the film is from Bazin's essay.

to the task but also it does not permit an escape into acceptance of occasional, inevitable, individual malfunctions of the system.

De Sica tries to condition in the spectator a protest which the case of Antonio Ricci does not indelibly warrant, and then he abstracts his tenuous argument into inaction. This conceptual insecurity in *Bicycle Thieves* leads to interpretative confusion. Bazin calls it, ' the only worthwhile Communist film made during the last ten years,'[3] but De Sica takes great care to point out that, '. . . film makers, when they depict human social problems, instinctively seek the causes and effects of the disequilibrium in human relationships. They are led to conclusions, a sort of commentary in images, which are more or less partisan. There is none of this in my work.'[4] Bazin says that it is partisan. De Sica says it's descriptive. If it is purely informational, that is, unemployment exists and robs man of his humanity and dignity, the film is dishonest to its meaningful stance. The spectator is tormented with imperatives by a declarative. If, as Bazin suggests, the film is overtly political, it is difficult to see any implied or stated political solution in the film.

Zavattini most adequately justifies *Bicycle Thieves* when he recalls, ' After *Bicycle Thieves,* De Sica and I, felt the need to go further, do something else, say more . . . We described things as they are. Now we must go beyond this stage, which was necessary in Italy, of simple protest.'[5] The aesthetic posture has in itself a political significance, but it is only a preliminary and incomplete consciousness — one which takes note of the aesthetic and social perversity imbedded in the system by tradition but which does not question the larger formal and political structures. Such an analysis suggests an

---

[3] p. 49, André Bazin, *op. cit.*

[4] p. 51, Pierre Leprohon, *Vittorio De Sica,* Cinéma d'Aujourd-hui 39, Editions Seghers, Paris, 1966.

[5] In an interview with Claude Roy, *Cahiers du Cinéma,* December 1951.

explanation for the film's final sequence, which has been subjected to a multitude of interpretations, all of which struggle to find significance in the resolution of a problem that is barely posed in the rest of the film. The primitive *prise de conscience* has exhausted itself before the film has finished. Bruno's irrelevant acceptance of his father's imperfections and Antonio's unnecessary realisation of his son's elevation to equal partnership in life's injustices demonstrate the film's inconclusive resolution.

The artefact which pretends not to be one is self-defeating, and the real world continues after ' The End.'

SIMON HARTOG   .

CREDITS

Original Italian title	Ladri di Biciclette
Produced by	P.D.S. (Produzioni De Sica)
Original story by	Cesare Zavattini
From the novel by	Luigi Bartolini
Script by	Oreste Biancoli, Suso Cecchi d'Amico, Vittorio De Sica, Adolfo Franci, Gherardo, Gherardi, Gerardo Guerrieri
Directed by	Vittorio De Sica
Photography by	Carlo Montuori
Edited by	Eraldo da Roma
Assistant director	Gerardo Guerrieri
Cameraman	Mario Montuori
Music by	Alessandro Cicognini
Orchestral director	Willy Ferrero
Décor	Antonino Traverso
Production manager	Umberto Scarpelli
Time	1 hour, 30 minutes
Process	Black and white

CAST

Antonio Ricci	Lamberto Maggiorani
Bruno Ricci	Enzo Staiola
Maria Ricci	Lianella Carell
Others	Elena Altieri, Gino Saltamerenda, Vittorio Antonucci, Guilio Chiari, Michele Sakara, Carlo Jachino, Nando Bruno, Fausto Guerzoni, Umberto Spadaro, Massimo Randisi

11

BICYCLE THIEVES

Titles superimposed over opening shot. Music : a swelling emotional, orchestral theme which returns in many of the dramatic moments throughout the film.
CITTA VALMELIANA: a drab, austere, dirty, but architecturally modern, government housing project for working class people on the outskirts of Rome. It is about 1946.
A bus, filled to overflowing, drives through the tedious rows of multi-storey buildings towards the camera. On this dry and sunny day the dust rises from the dirt-track road as the bus pulls up to release its flow of passengers. Pan with the crowd as they rush across the barren landscape and up a flight of steps into an office lodged in a massive wall. Almost immediately, they come out of the office, rush down the stairs, and wait anxiously together at the foot of the steps. A man, an official of sorts, with a little cigar in his mouth and a handful of papers, takes up his position facing the crowd on the stairs.

OFFICIAL *shouting*: Ricci . . . Ricci . . . Where's Ricci?
A MAN *in the crowd reacts. He moves through the crowd looking for* RICCI. *Camera tracks with him as he leaves the group, running and shouting.*

WORKER : Ricci . . . Ricci . . .
He runs towards the camera through the vast treeless expanse. An occasional poorly-dressed resident passes in the foreground.

WORKER : Ricci . . . Ricci . . .
RICCI, *sitting by a public fountain, looks up to see the* MAN *arrive.*

WORKER : Hey, Ricci . . . Are you deaf? They're calling you.

13

Come on. Quick.

>ANTONIO RICCI *gets up. Pan with the two men as they dash towards the distant crowd.* RICCI *momentarily dissolves into the crowd. The* OFFICIAL *is protesting.*

VOICE *off* : And what about me? I'm a mason. Must I die of hunger?

OFFICIAL : Look . . . What can I do? It's not my fault if there aren't enough jobs.

>RICCI *arrives a few steps below the* OFFICIAL.

OFFICIAL *continuing* : Damn it . . . Be a bit patient. We'll try to take care of everyone. That's what I'm here for. *Looking down at his papers.* But there's no mason on the list . . And now where's Ricci?

RICCI : Here.

OFFICIAL : I've a job for you.

RICCI *joyously* : A job for me?

OFFICIAL : Yes . . . Bill poster.

>*He takes some papers from his pocket and hands* RICCI *a card.*

OFFICIAL : Report to the Poster Office and give them this.

>RICCI *takes the paper and glances at it, unbelievingly.*

OFFICIAL *softly* : And make sure you take your papers with you.

RICCI *happy, muttering to himself* : I've been out of work so long . . .

VOICE *from the crowd* : What about me?

OFFICIAL : I still have two jobs for turners . . . but there aren't any turners here.

VOICE *again* : So, because I'm not a turner, I have to rot.

OFFICIAL *waving his bits of paper* : Yes . . . Yes . . . I know it's all my fault. *Turns towards* RICCI. Hey, Ricci.

>RICCI *has started to go down the steps towards the crowd. He stops and turns around.*

OFFICIAL : Don't forget to report with a bicycle.

>RICCI *looks worriedly at the paper in his hand.*

OFFICIAL *off* : It's written there. See?

14

RICCI *confused* : I've got a bike . . . but I haven't . . . I can get it in a few days.
OFFICIAL : That's no good. You've got to have it now. If not, no job.
RICCI : It can't be that important. I can walk for a few days.
OFFICIAL : Let's get this straight, Ricci. Do you, or don't you, have this bicycle? If you don't, I'll give the job to someone else.
MAN *in crowd* : Hey . . . I've got a bike.
ANOTHER : You're not the only one. I've got one too.
VOICES : Everyone's got one . . . Give me the job . . . I've got one too . . . So have I . . . Come on, give us your job.
OFFICIAL *almost screaming* : But you're a mason. This is another category.
MAN : Well, then, change my category.
OFFICIAL : No, you have to stay where you are. Well, Ricci, have you got one or not?
RICCI : Yes . . . Don't worry. I'll be there with it tomorrow morning.
> *He starts to leave.*
OFFICIAL : Listen . . . Don't try to fool us. If you turn up without it, it's no good.
RICCI *descending the steps* : And be out of work for another few years . . . I'll be there with the bicycle. I'll be there with it.
> *The* OFFICIAL *consults his list again.* RICCI *walks through the crowd towards the camera. Pan with him as he walks off, towards the buildings.*
OFFICIAL *off* : Is Cataldi here?
CATALDI *off* : Yes . . .
OFFICIAL *off* : There's a labourer's job for two days at the Tufelio site if you're interested.
CATALDI *off* : Of course, I'm interested. I'll take it.
> *The discussion is drowned as* RICCI *disappears behind a corner of a building in the distance. Dissolve.*
> *Track back with* RICCI *running along the side of a*

building towards the camera. He comes out into an
open space, and runs up to a wire fence. On the other
side of the fence, women are lined up waiting their turn
at the fountain.

RICCI: Maria . . . Hey . . . Maria.

A dark, modestly dressed woman in the crowd looks up
while the others gabble and gesticulate.

VOICES: Come on, it's my turn . . . What are you doing?
. . . No, it's mine.

Pan with MARIA *carrying two pails of water towards the*
fence until she arrives in front of RICCI.

MARIA: What is it? What's the matter?

RICCI: Oh, I've had pretty rotten luck . . .

MARIA: What's wrong, Antonio?

RICCI: I've got a job, but I can't take it.

RICCI walks away towards the buildings. MARIA *follows,*
having difficulty with the cumbersome pails. She tries
vainly to catch up. (Still on page 1)

MARIA: Wait, will you? What did you say? I didn't understand . . . You've a job? What is it? Tell me, Antonio.

RICCI *turning towards her*: It's good too. For the City.

He walks off again. MARIA *stumbles at the top of an*
incline. He walks back and takes one of the pails from
her, and they continue to walk, side by side. In the
background a group of children are playing. Track back
with the couple. (Still on page 1)

MARIA: What's wrong? Can't it be fixed?

RICCI: What do you want to fix? I've got to have a bicycle.
If I report without it tomorrow, someone else'll get the job.

Cut to the entrance hall of one of the squalid buildings.
They walk towards the hall and stop on the threshold.
MARIA *puts her pail down.*

MARIA: What are we going to do?

RICCI: What can we do?

A WOMAN *comes out from the building's shadowy stair-*
well and passes between them.

16

WOMAN : Hello, Signora Ricci.

MARIA : Hello, Signora . . . You see, Antonio, I knew you shouldn't have pawned your bike.

MARIA *picks up the pail and walks into the apartment building, towards the camera.* RICCI *raises his hands in frustration.*

RICCI : And how else could we have eaten?

MARIA *climbing the stairs* : Oh, shut up.

RICCI *following her* : Oh, why was I ever born!

MARIA : Enough, huh . . .

RICCI : I can always throw myself into the river . . .

MARIA : Enough!

Once on the landing, they go into their apartment and the door shuts behind them.

RICCI, *stands near the door of their apartment, pail in hand. Pan and track with* MARIA *who walks down the tiny corridor and places her pail on the kitchen table. In silence, she walks back and takes the pail from her husband. He goes into the bedroom and sits on the edge of the bed. Behind him are two family photographs: one has a black ribbon across it.* MARIA *comes in, squats down and opens the bottom drawer of the dresser. She takes out a paper-wrapped package and puts it on the table. She approaches* RICCI *and pulls at his arms.*

MARIA : Get up, Antonio.

Puzzled, he does as he is told, and watches MARIA *throw the blankets aside and gather up the sheets.*

RICCI : But what are you doing?

MARIA *with the sheets in her arms* : We can sleep without sheets, can't we? (*Still on page 2*)

Track, following her into the kitchen, where she throws the sheets into the corner and proceeds to fill a wash tub with water from a pail. Dissolve.

Inside a municipal pawnshop, some sheets are being pushed over a counter towards an EMPLOYEE. MARIA *looks anxiously through the counter window at his reac-*

17

tion. Facing the camera, the EMPLOYEE *examines the sheets, carefully.*

MARIA *off*: Sheets . . . six of them. They are linen . . . linen and cotton . . . good material . . . from my trousseau.

EMPLOYEE: They are used.

MARIA: Four are used. Two are new.

EMPLOYEE: How many are there?

MARIA: Three for a double bed and three for a single.

EMPLOYEE: . . . and three . . . *He pushes the sheets to one side and thinks* . . . Seven thousand lire.

MARIA *disappointed*: Seven thousand!

She looks round and steps back, and RICCI *comes forward to the window.*

RICCI: Can't you do any better?

EMPLOYEE: They're used . . . they're used . . .

MARIA *and* RICCI *look hopefully through the window. (Still on page 19)*

The EMPLOYEE *pushes the sheets towards a helper.*

EMPLOYEE: All right . . . put this stuff away. *He turns back to the couple.* Seven thousand, five hundred.

They both smile.

EMPLOYEE *writing*: What's the name?

MARIA: Ricci . . . Maria Ricci . . . Valmeliana, Building I, Staircase H.

EMPLOYEE: . . . Building I, Staircase H.

He puts his pen down, hands MARIA *a receipt, and takes a pile of banknotes.*

EMPLOYEE: One, two, three, four, five . . . *off, camera on* MARIA . . . six, seven. And one, two, three, four, five hundred. There you are.

MARIA *taking the money*: Thank you . . . Good-bye.

They move away from the window. An old man comes forward and regretfully places a pair of binoculars on the counter.

Another counter window is opened by another employee. Behind him rows of suspended bicycles. RICCI's *smiling*

18

face appears at the window. He hands the man a pawn ticket. The EMPLOYEE *takes it, checks it against his register, and looks up at* RICCI.

EMPLOYEE : Six thousand, one hundred.

RICCI *slightly surprised* : Why?

EMPLOYEE : The interest.

RICCI : Oh . . . *handing him the money* . . . Here . . .

The man, with the ticket in his hand, walks back to the stored bicycles. With obvious disinterest he glances from one to another. RICCI *watches him through the counter window.*

RICCI : It's a Fides . . . there . . . next to the red one.

EMPLOYEE : Yes, yes . . . I know . . . I know . . .

He walks further down the row. In the foreground, a man with a bundle of sheets, passes. Pan with him until he reaches a beehive of shelves filled from floor to ceiling with sheets. With some skill he climbs about half-way up the wall of shelves where he deposits the newly arrived bundle. RICCI *watches the man store his pawned goods. The man starts to climb down.*

A glass door opens onto the corridor of the municipal pawn shop. The EMPLOYEE *comes through it pushing the bike.* RICCI *advances towards the bike and takes feverish hold of it. The* EMPLOYEE *rudely grabs the bike back.*

EMPLOYEE : Hold it a second!

He removes a tag from the bicycle and then leaves. Pan with RICCI *as he pushes the bike towards the crowded entrance hall, where* MARIA *awaits him. Medium close-up of the happy couple. Dissolve.*

RICCI, *bicycle on his shoulder, walks up the stairs of the Poster Office. Pan with him as he walks down the dim corridor, its walls covered with many various posters. A man carrying a ladder walks by him.* RICCI *walks towards a man standing near a desk.*

RICCI : Where's the boss, please?

MAN *pointing*: That way. Put your bike down in the corner there.

Pan with RICCI *still carrying the bike as he walks towards an open door. He enters a cluttered room presided over by a balding man. It is the* BOSS. *Medium shot of the* BOSS *looking over the top of his glasses at the door.*

BOSS: Put that bike down . . .

RICCI *taking the bike off his shoulder*: I'm Ricci . . . Antonio Ricci. The Labour Officer at Valmeliana sent me.

He takes the card from his pocket; but he is intimidated and does not move. Camera cuts to a medium shot of the BOSS, *consulting a ledger.*

While reading it, he signals for RICCI *to come forward.*

BOSS: Ah, yes . . . here we are.

RICCI, *now pushing his bike, moves forward. The* BOSS *is seen in profile,* RICCI *in close-up.*

BOSS: You'll start in the morning. Now go to the stores and pick up your things.

RICCI *leaning forward respectfully*: Yes . . . thank you.

Long shot of RICCI *who puts on his hat and walks with his bike towards the door, where a man is standing.*

RICCI: Bye.

MAN: See you.

Dissolve.

Medium close-up of MARIA, *leaning against a wall in the street, waiting. Suddenly she smiles and runs out of shot. Long shot of* RICCI *with his bike and a large package, walking out of a large portico. He nods to the* PORTER.

PORTER: Tomorrow . . . at six-forty-five . . . all right?

RICCI: Yes . . . don't worry.

MARIA *walks into shot towards her husband. Medium close-up of them both.*

MARIA: How did it go?

RICCI: Oh . . . I'm sorry you had to wait, but it's all okay.

MARIA *looking happily at his bundle*: What's in there?

22

RICCI *handing her the package* : That's some work for you.
*Laughing, he takes off his hat and puts it on the package,
and takes out his official working cap. He puts it on. It
is a bit too large.*
RICCI : The band needs tightening.
MARIA looks at her husband with joy and admiration.
RICCI *smiling* : Does it suit me?
*She laughs while he puts the cap back into the package
and puts his old one on again. Pan with them as he
takes MARIA by the arm and leads her towards a barred
window.*
RICCI : Come here . . . I want to show you something.
*RICCI leans his bike against the wall, and lifts MARIA
up so that she can see through the window. (Still on page
19)*
RICCI : Look . . . Everyone has his own locker. Isn't it great?
*Someone inside slams the shutters closed. RICCI lets
MARIA down, and ties his package to the back of the
bike.*
RICCI : Just think . . . they used to give them shoes too . . .
Anyway, the pay is good. Six thousand every fortnight plus
family allowances . . . and overtime too. Let's go.
*Medium close-up as RICCI gets on the bike and MARIA
on the handlebars.*
MARIA : Oh . . . Antonio, can we stop in Via della Paglia for
a minute?
RICCI *surprised* : What do you want to do there?
MARIA : Nothing . . . I just want to see a woman there.
RICCI *with ironic jealousy* : A woman?
MARIA : Yes . . . a woman.
*They ride off, out of shot. Long shot of the street with
their backs to the camera, the bike's bell tinkling. Long
shot of another street. They arrive at the kerb near the
entrance to a building. RICCI puts his feet to the ground
as MARIA jumps off.*
MARIA : It's here . . . wait for me.

RICCI : Who lives here?

MARIA *hurriedly* : I've already told you. *Moving towards the door.* I'll be out in a minute.

RICCI : But . . .?

MARIA *returning a few steps* : But I'll be right back!

She moves towards the interior staircase while RICCI *wedges his bike against the wall. He looks up towards his wife.*

RICCI : Hurry up.

Low angle shot of MARIA, *climbing to the first landing and going through the half-open door. While surveying the street, standing near the entrance,* RICCI *takes a cigarette from his pocket and is about to light it. An adolescent* BOY *runs into shot next to the bike, closely followed by a series of stones which land near the front wheel. Then two more* BOYS *arrive.*

FIRST BOY : Look . . . it's mine.

SECOND BOY : No, it's mine.

RICCI gestures concurrence as he lights his cigarette.

SECOND BOY : All right . . . that makes five to three. We'll play another, huh? But this time . . .

RICCI smiles as they disappear, and then watches the approach of three sombrely dressed women, one of whom is in mourning. They enter the building and search for the concierge.

WOMEN *calling* : Signora . . . Signora . . . Is anyone here?

One of the WOMEN *comes towards* RICCI.

WOMAN : This is where Signora Santona lives, isn't it?

RICCI *not understanding* : Signora Santona?

WOMAN : Yes, the fortune teller.

RICCI : I'm afraid I don't live here.

WOMAN *walking back towards the stairs with her friends:* We'll try upstairs.

RICCI follows their climb with considerable curiosity. Low angle shot of the landing as the WOMEN *arrive and, following* MARIA'S *path, go into the apartment. High*

24

angle shot of RICCI *who has come half-way up the stairs to see where the* WOMEN *have gone. In the background, the* BOYS *with their stone game have reappeared near the entrance.*

BOY : It's mine again.

ANOTHER : Wait . . . we'll measure.

RICCI *turns to watch their deliberations as a* WOMAN *comes out of the* SANTONA *apartment, mopping her tear-streaked face with a handkerchief. She passes* RICCI *who watches her go down the stairs and out the door.*

RICCI *to the* BOYS : Hey . . . watch my bike, will you.

BOY : Yes . . . all right.

RICCI *climbs to the landing and enters the door.*

RICCI *sidles timidly past the half-open door into* SIGNORA SANTONA'S *apartment; he walks cautiously down the corridor, towards the camera. Medium shot in profile of* RICCI, *who arrives in front of an open door through which a young* WOMAN *can be seen working near a stove.*

WOMAN *without turning* : The end door . . .

Track in to a medium close-up of RICCI, *who takes off his hat and continues down the corridor. A barely audible conversation filters from the end room.*

SIGNORA SANTONA *off* : How is he now?

WOMAN *off* : He's been ill for almost a year.

SIGNORA SANTONA *off* : You could call a doctor.

WOMAN *off* : I did, but he said that nothing could be done.

SIGNORA SANTONA *off* : You should have brought him to me.

WOMAN *off* : How could I? . . . He can't move . . . Do something . . . I beg you . . .

RICCI *creeps up to a door at the end of the corridor and stands there, half-hidden. Through the door is the fortune teller's room with its middle-class furnishings, religious pictures and votive lights. Next to the large bed sits* SIGNORA SANTONA, *pontificating in her dressing gown, with a young* ASSISTANT *by her side. The room is crowded with people, mostly women, who have come to consult her.* SIGNORA SANTONA *raises her hands towards heaven and joins them.*

ASSISTANT, *indicating the next customer, with a hand-waving ritual* : This one yes, that one no.

SIGNORA SANTONA : Give me light, My Lord . . . Give me the light . . .

Medium close-up of RICCI *peering nervously through the door. A longer shot of* SIGNORA SANTONA *and her clients.*

SIGNORA SANTONA : You son will rise from his bed before the leaves fall.

WOMAN : What does that mean?

RICCI *recognizes* MARIA *among the people in the room.*

RICCI *in a very low voice* : Maria!

MARIA *turns her head towards the door and looks annoyed.*

SIGNORA SANTONA *off* : That means that your son will be better by the autumn.

RICCI : Maria . . . are you coming?

MARIA *irritably shrugs ' No '.*

WOMAN *off* : Oh, thank you . . . thank you.

RICCI *becoming angry* : Let's go, Maria.

SIGNORA SANTONA *off* : Now what can I do for you?

ANOTHER WOMAN *off* : I've my sister-in-law ill.

RICCI : Maria!

SIGNORA SANTONA *off* : God, give me light . . . Give me the light.

In medium shot, MARIA *walks towards her husband and the camera, to avoid a scene. She is furious. Track back as she leaves the room closing the door behind her. Medium close-up of them both in the corridor.*

RICCI *shoving his wife down the corridor* : Come on . . . What are you doing here, anyway?

MARIA : Nothing . . . I had to give her fifty lire.

RICCI *as if to a child* : Silly fool . . .

MARIA : Listen, she said you'd find a job. You found one . . . Yes? So I've got to pay her.

RICCI: Do you want me to go in there and tell her what I think?

MARIA *taking him by the arm*: All right ... Let's go.

Track with them as they walk towards the exit.

RICCI *a little calmer*: How can you, a woman with two children and with a head on your shoulders, be taken in by this foolishness ... these frauds ... As if these witches had any control over people's lives ... It's just idiotic.

As they pass the kitchen door MARIA furtively puts some money on the table. The WOMAN in the kitchen watches her, but says nothing. MARIA catches up with RICCI, takes his hand gently, and leads him to the door. From the bottom of the stairwell they are seen coming down the stairs.

RICCI: Haven't you got anything better to spend your money on?

MARIA: But I'm grateful ...

RICCI: It shouldn't be allowed ...

They come out of the building into the street. The camera tracks back with them as they arrive on the pavement. RICCI, still muttering, pushes the bike onto the road and gets on. MARIA gets up onto the handlebars.

RICCI *now jocular*: And who found this job then? Her or me? Let's go home, silly.

He pushes off. Dissolve.

In another shot they are seen riding towards the camera. Fade to black.

Medium long shot of the children's room in RICCI's apartment, early next morning. Close-up of a suspended bicycle wheel turning. Through the spokes, BRUNO, RICCI's son who is about ten, is seen polishing the bike with great care. RICCI, in his uniform, enters the room.

RICCI: Hurry up, Bruno ... It's six-thirty. (*Still on page 20*)

BRUNO: I can't clean it very well in here. It's too dark still.

Pan with BRUNO as he walks to the window and opens the shutters onto the feeble morning light. Pan back to

27

the bike with him. RICCI *moves towards his son. Medium close-up of* BRUNO, *polishing a pedal and looking unhappy.*

BRUNO : Papa . . . did you see what they did?

RICCI *off* : No . . . What?

BRUNO *furiously points to the pedal* : A dent!

RICCI, *in medium shot, sits smiling on the bed to tie his laces.*

RICCI : Perhaps it was there before . . .

BRUNO *enraged* : No . . . it wasn't . . . I'm sure. You don't know how they look after things in there? You should have been more careful . . . It's not them who pays for repairs, you know.

RICCI *laughing* : Shhh . . . keep quiet.

BRUNO *cleaning and sulking* : I'll keep quiet, but I'd have complained to them.

In the corridor, RICCI, *doing up his belt, comes towards the camera in the direction of the kitchen. Pan with him as he walks up to* MARIA, *who is adjusting the cap's band by the window. They are seen together in medium shot.*

RICCI : You almost finished?

MARIA : Yes.

RICCI *turns towards the table and eyes the two packets lying there: one is longer than the other.*

MARIA *getting up* : Pasta.

MARIA *puts the cap on her husband's head.*

MARIA : Hmm . . . let's see. You look handsome.

RICCI : It's true. I'm handsome.

MARIA *smiling* : You look like a policeman.

She laughs as he feigns a slap, and then shakes her head lovingly. They embrace. She pulls herself away and while arranging her hair, scolds him jokingly.

MARIA : Go on . . . get going. You hurt me . . . You're going to wake the baby.

He kisses her on the cheek, picks up the lunch packets,

28

and leaves. Fade to black.

Medium long shot of the children's room. BRUNO comes in followed by his father. He gives BRUNO his lunch bag.

RICCI: Here's your omelette, Bruno.

BRUNO proudly imitating his father, puts his lunch into the front pocket of his overalls. He turns and combs his hair. RICCI goes out of shot. BRUNO picks up his scarf and throws it round his neck. RICCI reappears, with the bike on his shoulder, straightening his cap in the mirror one last time. He starts towards the door.

RICCI: Let's go, Bruno.

As his father leaves the room, BRUNO looks towards the other end of the room. Shot of the baby lying wedged between two pillows on a bed. BRUNO changes his mind, retraces his steps, and closes the shutters, plunging the room into darkness.

RICCI walks out to the landing outside the apartment, carrying his bike. BRUNO is following him. They both turn back to MARIA, out of shot.

BRUNO: Bye, mama.

RICCI *smiling*: Bye.

MARIA *off*: Bye.

RICCI shuts the door, and the screen fades to black.

The first faint glimmers of dawn are showing over the city outside. A crowded tram passes. Workers, many on bicycles, move through the streets. Among the cyclists, RICCI rides with BRUNO on the handlebars. Long shot of a street leading to Porta Pingiana, the cyclists are back lit by the morning light. RICCI pulls up at the kerb of a still deserted piazza. A bus pulls up and disgorges its human wave. BRUNO descends from his perch.

RICCI: I'll pick you up tonight at seven . . . Wait for me here . . . all right?

RICCI starts off. BRUNO, with his back to camera, watches his father ride away.

BRUNO: Bye, papa . . . Bye . . .

Pan with BRUNO as he climbs some steps. A MAN is busy sweeping them.

BRUNO: Morning.

The MAN does not return the greeting. BRUNO enters a small shed and comes out with a jerry can and a funnel, which he puts on the ground next to a petrol pump.

Track back with RICCI in medium close-up as he pedals down a shadowy street. Dissolve.

A mass of cyclists, ladders on their shoulders, stream out of the Poster Office. As they ride off to work, the only other workers in the streets are the street sweepers and the rubbish collectors. Dissolve.

The sunlight is now bright. RICCI and a COLLEAGUE are standing in front of a poster-covered wall. The man unfolds a section of a poster and walks towards the wall. RICCI follows with a pail of glue. In the background, their bikes rest against the wall. Pan and track forward onto the COLLEAGUE who explains as he pastes up the poster.

COLLEAGUE: See ... First you put some paste on the wall like this ... then you stick the poster up ... make sure it's straight ... and cover it with a light coat of glue ...

Medium long shot of the two MEN at the wall. Near them two kids, one playing an accordion. The poster is for a Rita Hayworth film ...

COLLEAGUE *continuing*: That's so that when it dries there aren't any wrinkles ... *To the kids* ... Hey ... go play somewhere else ... *to* RICCI ... if you leave any wrinkles, and the inspector sees them, you're out of a job ...

An elderly man passes them with his back to the camera. He is elegantly dressed in a black hat and coat; he carries a briefcase under his arm, and uses an umbrella as a cane. Pan with him as he walks down the street. One of the boys follows him hoping to get some money, but comes back empty handed.

COLLEAGUE *off*: ... You see ... for this job, Ricci, you've

30

got to be intelligent : have a good eye and be alert.

The two men take their ladders and walk to the bikes.

COLLEAGUE : Well, that's that one done.

They get on their bikes and get ready to set off in different directions.

COLLEAGUE : I'll leave you now . . . See you.

RICCI : Thanks . . . Bye.

Pan with RICCI *as he rides down the street. Dissolve. A street in the centre of the city. Close-up of the Rita Hayworth poster with air bubbles showing all over it.* RICCI'S *hands come into shot as he attempts to smooth out the poster. Noise of heavy traffic.* RICCI *is working on a wall already covered and recovered with posters of all sizes and types. (Still on page 37) The bike stands on the pavement near the foot of* RICCI'S *ladder and glue pot. Three, rather suspicious looking* MEN, *amble non-chalantly along the pavement away from the camera. They hesitate for a moment near the bicycle and then continue on their way. They separate. One of them comes back towards the bike. Pan with the youngest, who drifts behind the parked cars. Keeping an eye on* RICCI, *he waits for the right moment.* RICCI *is still on the ladder busily trying to flatten out the poster. (Still on page 38) The young* MAN, *wearing a German forage cap and jacket, looks around, then walks towards his accomplice near the bike. They pay no attention to each other. The young* MAN *takes a final look towards* RICCI. *Cut to* RICCI *still working, then back to a medium shot of the young* MAN, *who jumps onto the bike. The glue pot clangs on the pavement, knocked over as he tears away down the street. Medium close-up of* RICCI *on the ladder as he turns.*

RICCI : Stop him ! Stop the thief !

RICCI *jumps down and dashes after the man on the zig-zagging bike.*

RICCI : Thief ! Thief !

RICCI *rushes along the pavement, bumps into the* ACCOM-

31

PLICE, *who has deliberately placed himself in* RICCI'S *path.*

ACCOMPLICE : What happened?

RICCI *pushes past the man, who then runs after him. Long shot of the street. The* THIEF *flashes by, with* RICCI *running and shouting behind him. Pan with* RICCI *as he arrives in a large open square. No one in the street pays much attention beyond vague, cursory glances at the chase.*

High angle shot of the square. The THIEF *loses himself in the traffic.* RICCI *runs up to a car that is moving in the same direction as the* THIEF.

RICCI *to the driver* : Stop him!

Seen from the back seat of the car, the DRIVER, *back to camera, waves to* RICCI *to get on the running board.*

DRIVER : Hurry . . . Come on . . . Get on.

RICCI *gets on and points* : Catch him . . . He went this way . . . Quick . . . Hurry.

Long shot of the square. As the car moves towards a tunnel, the ACCOMPLICE *also jumps on the running board on the other side of the car.*

ACCOMPLICE : The tunnel . . . I saw him . . . Go towards the tunnel.

Camera tracks forward from the front of the car, towards the tunnel and a cyclist wearing a cap and jacket. Medium shot of RICCI *on the running board.*

RICCI : Faster . . . Faster . . . We must catch him.

From the front, tracking forward, the car enters the tunnel. Long shot from inside the tunnel: the car, moving towards camera, cuts off the cyclist and forces him to stop. He is furious. Medium shot of the cyclist. He is not the THIEF. *Medium long shot of the car, the* ACCOMPLICE *jumping at the cyclist.*

CYCLIST : Hey, what's the matter with you?

The ACCOMPLICE *lets him go.*

CYCLIST : You crazy or something?

RICCI *is desolate as he sees the mistake and gets off the running board, stunned. Medium shot of the* CYCLIST *and the* ACCOMPLICE.

CYCLIST : Next time you'd better be more careful.

The CYCLIST *remounts his bike and leaves. Pan in medium close-up of the* ACCOMPLICE *who returns to the car in false bewilderment.*

ACCOMPLICE *to the driver* : I don't understand. I must have made a mistake . . . But I could have sworn he came this way . . .

DRIVER : Sure . . . sure . . . We know . . .

The ACCOMPLICE *shrugs his shoulders and moves off.* RICCI *is seen in long shot, running out of the tunnel into the square, back to camera. Low angle shot of* RICCI, *looking very worn, towards camera. He looks vainly round the square, and wipes the sweat from his forehead. Track back as he walks like a sleepwalker. (Still on page 39)*

RICCI : It's terrible . . . terrible !

Long shots of jammed streets are intercut with shots of RICCI *walking slowly back to his ladder. Music. He leans against the ladder for a few seconds, straightens up, and throws the glue pot noisily to the ground. He seems about to do the same with the ladder, but instead he takes his brush and irrelevantly strokes the poster with it, and then throws the brush down in desperation. Finally, he sits on the ladder to consider his fate. Camera tracks in on him. Dissolve.*

Medium close-up of RICCI *in a police station facing the camera with the posters under his arm. In the foreground, in close-up, a police officer. Behind him, shelves, desks, and people milling about.*

RICCI : Oh . . . yes. There were people . . . but they were minding their own business . . . Then I started to run . . .

MAN *off* : Hey . . . Failoni !

The officer, FAILONI, *who has been taking* RICCI'S *state-*

33

*ment, gets up and walks towards the open window
where the man is calling. Camera tracks with him as he
reaches the window and leans out.*

FAILONI: What?

*High angle onto the courtyard, in which a number of
jeeps filled with police stand ready to leave. The man
in charge looks up to the window.*

MAN: You have to go to the meeting.

FAILONI: Capece was supposed to go.

MAN: That's all been changed. Capece is going to Tiburtino
and you and Quadrone have to go instead.

*The MAN gets into one of the jeeps and they all roar off.
Pan with FAILONI coming back to the desk at which
RICCI is still sitting. RICCI looks up at FAILONI, as he is
given a paper.*

FAILONI: Sign there.

*While RICCI signs, FAILONI calls to a man in the back-
ground.*

FAILONI: Quadrone!

QUADRONE *off*: Yes, sir.

FAILONI: It's our turn . . .

QUADRONE *off*: Let's go right away then.

Shot of RICCI holding the statement he has just signed.

RICCI: Can something be done about it?

FAILONI: If you've got time you could try looking yourself.

FAILONI turns to get his coat. RICCI is bitter and worried.

RICCI: So I'm supposed to cover Rome all by myself?

FAILONI: Am I? I don't even know what it looks like.

RICCI: But I gave you the number and the description.

FAILONI *off*: Look . . . We'd need an entire mobile brigade to
find your bicycle.

RICCI: What about my statement. What's the use of that?

*FAILONI has his coat and hat on. Medium close-up of
them both.*

FAILONI: That can be useful. Suppose tomorrow you were to
find your bike in a shop or in the street, you could call a

34

policeman and you'd be in the right.

In the background, a man, notebook in his hand, approaches the desk.

JOURNALIST: Anything new, constable?

FAILONI: No, nothing . . . just a bicycle.

JOURNALIST *leaving*: Thanks . . . see you tonight.

RICCI: Well, then, I'm supposed to look after it myself?

FAILONI *getting angry*: That's enough! You've filed your complaint . . . That's all. Good-bye.

RICCI: Good-bye.

The OFFICER walks off. RICCI, crestfallen, turns and slowly moves towards the exit. Dissolve.

Music. It is now dusk. In a piazza in the city the camera makes a long lateral track on a bus queue: the people there are noisy and numerous, until a bus swallows up some of the crowd. The doors shut, and it drives off. Camera tracks in on the people waiting for the next bus. The people push against each other, grumbling angrily.

VOICES: Hey! Go to the back like everyone else . . . Don't push. I was first . . . It's always the same thing . . . Careful!

As RICCI, recognisable by his official cap, edges his way forward in the queue, he is jostled and maligned by a woman next to him. He manages to squeeze into the next bus just before the doors close, leaving those remaining outside to demonstrate their dissatisfaction with even greater venom. Dissolve.

Camera cuts to a long shot of the piazza at Porta Pia, Monte Sacro. It is night. Pan across to BRUNO standing alone, next to the petrol pump.

RICCI *off*: Hey . . . Bruno!

Startled, BRUNO turns as his father comes into shot. Medium close-up of them both.

BRUNO: Papa . . . it's half-past seven.

RICCI: I came on the bus . . . Let's go.

They walk towards the camera and it tracks back with

them.

Bruno *hestitantly* : What about the bicycle?

Ricci *looks icily at his son and continues walking. Camera cuts to a long shot of another piazza on the outskirts of the city. Father and son walk away from the camera in the distance. A bus passes behind them. Long shot of small groups of workers crossing a bridge, among them Ricci and Bruno. In a slight high angle shot, the camera tracks back in medium close-up, to show the two of them still walking in uneasy silence.*

Bruno *anxiously* : Is it broken?

Ricci *irritably* : Yes. It's broken.

They continue on in silence. Ricci rearranges Bruno's scarf without stopping. Dissolve.

Cut to Ricci and his son, climbing the stairs, and stopping in front of their apartment door. Slight tilt up from the stairs in mid-shot as Ricci noiselessly opens the door and lets Bruno enter.

Ricci : Go in . . . I'll be along later. Go on . . . go in.

Ricci closes the door behind Bruno and softly walks down the stairs towards camera. Cut to a long shot of the housing estate at night. Ricci walks quickly towards one of the buildings.

Ricci hurries down the steps of a stucco stairwell. Track back with him as he enters a vast but dimly lit cellar, sprinkled with labyrinthine vaulted corridors . . . It is the Party Headquarters.

Speaker *off* : It's impossible to find jobs for people, since there's no work. We, as a cell, have pointed this out to the Labour Office. And, we know, the dole is not the answer.

Ricci comes into the area where the discussion is taking place, and moves towards the group standing silent and attentive. In the centre of the group, the Speaker gesticulates.

Speaker *continuing* : What we need is a big public building programme. And you heard what they said at the meeting

today . . . the same old things.

RICCI *is seen in medium close-up, edging his way through the people towards a familiar face, the* EMPLOYMENT OFFICIAL. *He whispers an unheard question.*

SPEAKER *to* RICCI : Hey . . . quiet please . . . If you don't want to listen to this, go somewhere else.

RICCI *quickly and softly finishes his question.*

RICCI : . . . Biaocco . . . Is he here?

The other MAN *does not reply. Track laterally with him as he turns and walks down one of the corridors.*

SPEAKER *off* : We are constantly trying to integrate you into the system, but you can't expect miracles . . .

The SPEAKER'S *voice is smothered by music coming from another part of the cellar.* RICCI, *in medium long shot, and back to camera, is seen going into the hall where the music is being played. In the background, on a tiny stage some amateur actors in their work clothes are rehearsing a number for a modest ' cabaret '. Near the stage, a pianist bangs out a few chords.* RICCI *goes into the room and sits on one of the benches in the back. Long shot from below of the stage, seen from* RICCI'S *point of view, where a man is singing in dialect, and off-key.*

SINGER : If you really love me
　　　　If you really love me . . .

The entrance to the room. A man enters and puts up a poster on the wall. He turns towards RICCI, *out of shot.*

MAN : Is it on straight?

RICCI *forcing a helpful smile and nodding* : Yes . . .

The SINGER *on stage seems overcome by the stupidity of his song. He stands, shrugs, and walks to the back of the stage where he joins the two-woman chorus. The ' producer ', a large, heavy-set man, walks up to them looking profoundly dissatisfied. Cut to* RICCI *who makes a sign to the ' producer ',* BIAOCCO.

BIAOCCO *to the actors* : Carry on without me. I'll be back in

a minute. *He gets off the stage and comes towards* RICCI.
. . . What is it?

> *Medium close-up of them both, as* BIAOCCO *sits down next to* RICCI.

RICCI : I was looking for you.

BIAOCCO : What's happened, Antonio?

RICCI *in close-up, emotionally* : My bike's been stolen.

BIAOCCO *in close-up* : No . . . Where?

RICCI : Fiorala . . . while I was putting up posters.

BIAOCCO : But how could you . . .

RICCI : Oh . . . Biaocco . . . you must help me. I must find that bike.

BIAOCCO : That's easy enough to say . . .

> *Long shot of the stage, the actors trying lamentably hard. The* SINGER *blames the women when he makes a mistake.*

SINGER : Stop! Stop! Biaocco, listen for a bit, otherwise we'll be here all night.

BIAOCCO *irritated* : I'm listening. I'm listening.

SINGER : If you really love me . . .

BIAOCCO *in medium close-up next to* RICCI : Listen! *Singing* . . . If you really love me. REALLY! REALLY! . . . It's a simple song. Go on. Try again!

> *Back on the stage, the pianist starts again, but the* SINGER *gives up in disgust. He sits on the edge of the stage while the others do a dance. Cut back to* BIAOCCO *and* RICCI.

BIAOCCO : The only thing to do is to go Piazza Vittorio very early. Thieves sell the bikes as quick as they can. They don't hide them at home. I think that's the best place to look.

> *Camera cuts to the entrance to the hall.* MARIA *is there, and the camera pans with her as she comes towards her husband.*

MARIA *aghast* : Antonio!

> *He turns towards her, upset by her presence. He looks at her for a moment, then gets to his feet.*

RICCI : Maria . . .

MARIA: Is it true?

RICCI: Look . . . I didn't come home so that I wouldn't have to listen to your moaning.

MARIA: Moaning? Who's moaning? . . . But there's good reason to with news like this . . . Have you done anything about it?

RICCI sits down again.

MARIA *off*: Have you looked for it?

BIAOCCO: Don't cry, Maria. You're acting like a child.

Close-up of MARIA drying her eyes.

BIAOCCO *off*: They'll change the seat and the handlebars, but it'll turn up at the market in the morning. And if it does, we'll bring it home . . . *to RICCI in medium shot* . . . Hey . . . Antonio . . . you'll miss a bit of sleep tonight, that's all. *Close-up of MARIA.* But the important thing is to find it. Come on, cheer up.

On the stage, one of the actors approaches the two actresses and bows.

ACTOR: Ladies. Would you be so kind as to tell me what you're doing tonight?

ACTRESS: I'm supposed to go for a walk with a girl friend.

ACTOR: You could come for a walk with me.

ACTRESS: No, my mother is coming too.

Cut to a long shot of the room from the stage. The discussion about politics in the other room has finished, and some of the participants have wandered into the rehearsal area. General hubbub. On the stage the SINGER is furious.

SINGER *to the people who have just come in*: Ah! No! No! That's it. Either you leave or we leave. . . . Well? . . . Hey, Maniconi, get them out of here.

The ACTOR, doing as he is asked, walks the length of the room and hustles the people towards the exit.

ACTOR: He's right. Come on, out. Let's rehearse.

BIAOCCO and RICCI get up and MARIA stands by them.

BIAOCCO: Good-night then. And don't get angry about it.

43

Ricci *and* Maria *together*: Good-night.
Biaocco *clasping his hands*: Everything'll be all right.

Camera cuts to a medium shot of Ricci *and his wife leaving the room with the rest. Camera tracks back in medium close-up as they walk down the corridor towards camera in silence. Track forward from behind them until they reach the stairs. Fade to black.*

A long shot of the Piazza Vittorio, almost obscured in the cloudy dawn light. The headlights and interior lights of a tram are still on. It stops and among those who descend are Ricci *and* Bruno. Ricci, *holding his son by the hand, walks quickly towards the camera. Even though the street lights go out, the light does not change. Day is timidly breaking. In the background are street sweepers with their wooden brooms, and parked along the kerb, lorries for rubbish collection. Track in to show a ladder on the back of one of the lorries upon which* Biaocco *is standing, directing the unloading of the street sweepers' carts into the lorry. He shouts to the driver, out of shot, to increase the speed of the lorry's rubbish compression.*

Biaocco: Give it more gas, Maniconi . . . otherwise we'll never get finished this morning . . . *Then to a street sweeper.* . . . What's that cart doing there . . . right in the middle? No one can get by. Move it away.

Bruno and Ricci *come into shot.*

Ricci: Hey . . . Biaocco!
Biaocco: All right, here I am. *He climbs down and comes to join them where they stand in the foreground.* Hey, Maniconi, Bagonghi! Come over here . . . *To* Ricci . . . By the way, what make was it?
Bruno *excitedly*: Fides . . . a Fides frame!
Ricci: You can see he knows it better than I do!
Biaocco *patting* Bruno *affectionately on the head*: That's good! *To everyone.* Because they take everything to bits at this place. We'll have to split up. Bagonghi, you come with me.

44

We'll go to the sheltered side of the market. You go and check the tyres. You'll be looking at the frames. *He indicates who is to have each job. (Still on page 40)*

BAGONGHI : Uh huh!

BIAOCCO : The kid can look at the bells and pumps. *To* BRUNO. Understand, eh?

MANICONI *to* BAGONGHI : Remember, it's a Fides frame.

BAGONGHI *shrugging his shoulders* : Okay, okay, I know.

The square is seen in long shot as the group moves forward in the general direction of camera. BIAOCCO *is in the lead, followed by* RICCI, BRUNO *and* MANICONI. *Long shot of the group walking forward.*

BIAOCCO : We'll have to look for it piece by piece. Then, when we've found all the bits, we'll put it together again. *Shot of them from behind.* We'll have to look through all the stalls. *In the background, the stalls of the street market are being prepared for the morning's activities. The group turns towards the market area.*

BIAOCCO : Don't look like a team of investigators. Be indifferent!

Some men are seen in long shot coming through an archway, pushing a mass of bicycles towards the stalls. (Still on page 39) The group enters shot and looks at the passing bikes.

MANICONI : I'm sure we'll find it.

BIAOCCO *pointing* : Let's go that way . . .

Camera tracks with them as they walk. They stop again for a moment.

BIAOCCO *to* BRUNO : You go and look at the bells and pumps, Bruno. Don't worry about anything else. Understand? If you find something, whistle. That's the way to do it!

RICCI *and his son are seen in medium close-up.*

RICCI *leaning towards* BRUNO : Look carefully . . . and if you find it we'll really celebrate.

BIAOCCO : Don't worry. He's a smart boy. You coming, Antonio?

Lateral track with BRUNO *as the others go in the opposite direction.*

VOICES *mostly off*: Bianchi 25, Bianchi 25! A brand new article . . . Look here, gentlemen . . . Only three days old . . .

In the foreground, two men are putting the finishing touches to their spare parts stall. In the background, on the other side of the stall, facing the camera, BRUNO *interestedly examines one of the items on the stall.*

SALESMAN *pushing him*: Hey. Don't touch. Push off.

Cut to a shot of MANICONI *and* BAGONGHI *walking round together.*

MANICONI: Come on, Bagonghi, wake up . . . look for a Fides!

Camera tracks back with the group, who are still going round. In the background, two men with folding tables, piled high with loose tobacco, are arguing about who has the right to that particular selling position. Shots of stacked bikes, other stalls, and tyres.

BIAOCCO *off*: Let's split up. It's pointless to stay together like this.

Music. Camera tracks back to a medium close-up of RICCI *looking round.* MANICONI, *the same.* BRUNO, *the same.* BIAOCCO, *the same. Shots of bikes and frames in the stalls. Camera cranes back and up to a high angle of the market. Cut back to the group.* MANICONI *comes running up and starts to drag* BIAOCCO *back with him.*

MANICONI: Quick . . . Come and look at this frame.

BRUNO, *alone, is looking at some bells. The others arrive in front of a stall where a man is repainting a frame. (Still on page 40)*

PAINTER: You want something?

RICCI: What make is that?

PAINTER *aggressively*: Why? . . . You want to buy it?

RICCI *in close-up*: No. *He leans forward.*

PAINTER *seen from above*: Don't touch that! The paint's still wet.

RICCI: I only wanted to see the registration number.

46

PAINTER: And why do you want to do that? Perhaps you want to buy the number?

Cut to a general shot of the group.

BIAOCCO: No, we don't want to buy the number, but we want to see it.

PAINTER: And if I don't want to let you see it ―― ?

RICCI: Then I'll go and get a policeman and we'll see . . .

PAINTER *furious*: Go and get whoever you want . . .

Low angle of RICCI, *his mind made up, as he turns and walks away.*

PAINTER *worried*: Anyway . . . this bike isn't stolen, understand?

BIAOCCO: Nobody says it is . . . but you're obliged to show the number . . .

A WOMAN *comes rushing hysterically from the back of the stall.*

WOMAN: No, I won't show you the number!

PAINTER *in close-up*: What do you want with the number anyway? To play the lottery?

BIAOCCO: No . . . I never play the lottery.

Cut back to BRUNO, *still looking at the bells. An elderly man comes up to him, and studies him carefully. He is obviously a homosexual. He leans towards the boy.*

OLD MAN: Do you want to buy the bell, the pretty bell? You've been looking at it for such a long time.

BRUNO *moves away but the* OLD MAN *follows.*

OLD MAN: No . . . you don't want it? Of course, you do . . . *To the salesman* . . . How much is it?

SALESMAN: 150 lire . . .

OLD MAN *to* BRUNO: Wouldn't you like it?

BRUNO *shakes his head.*

Cut back to the others facing the PAINTER. RICCI *arrives with a* POLICEMAN.

POLICEMAN: If you've filed a complaint, that's enough . . . *To the* PAINTER. Let's see the frame.

PAINTER *holding the frame up*: Look at it as much as you

47

want . . . One can't be left to work in peace any more . . .

The POLICEMAN *holds the frame up to find the registration number.* RICCI *leans forward to look too.*

POLICEMAN *to* RICCI : Don't you trust me? *Reading the
number with difficulty.* Twelve, zero, twenty-four . . .

RICCI *is very disappointed.*

POLICEMAN *off* : And is it yours?

RICCI *shaking his head* : No.

Pan with the POLICEMAN *as he hands the frame back to
the* PAINTER, *who has regained his composure, and who
hands the* POLICEMAN *a cloth.*

PAINTER : Here . . . you got yourself dirty for nothing!

The POLICEMAN *wipes the paint off his hands with the
cloth.*

RICCI *very sad* : It wasn't that I didn't trust you . . . but if a
bloke has his bike stolen, he at least has a right to look . . .

PAINTER *harshly* : Look . . . No one's stopping you.

POLICEMAN : Anyone can make a mistake.

*He hands back the cloth and walks off, while the others
watch him. Medium long shot of the group, back to
camera; in the foreground, the* PAINTER *looks towards
them.*

PAINTER : Well . . . we all know that in Piazza Vittorio there's
nothing but *honest* people.

MANICONI *and the* PAINTER *exchange vicious looks.*

BAGONGHI : Come on, that's enough. Don't bother.

*Camera tracks laterally with the group, as they move
away from the stall. They arrive at the other stall where*
BRUNO *is still being pestered by the* OLD MAN.

OLD MAN : Would you like something else then?

RICCI *takes his son by the hand.*

RICCI : Bruno, don't wander off like that. Let's go.

The OLD MAN *looks very put out as they walk out of
shot.*

*Cut back to a long shot of the street, the group returns
towards the lorries, their hopes somewhat dampened.*

48

BIAOCCO *to* RICCI: Why not try Porta Portese? Maniconi can drive you there. We'll stay here . . . you never know.

Track in to frame them in front of a lorry.

MANICONI: I don't know . . . I think it's better here . . . We should have gone to Porta Portese earlier this morning.

BIAOCCO *helping* BRUNO *and* RICCI *into the lorry*: Take them anyway . . . no harm in trying.

MANICONI: All right . . . I don't mind.

He walks in front of the lorry and climbs into the driver's seat while BIAOCCO *closes the passengers' door.*

BIAOCCO: Off you go . . . drive slowly.

The lorry moves away down the street, seen in long shot. BIAOCCO and BAGONGHI walk back towards the market. Long shot of the lorry moving down an empty street, the stormy sky making it unusually dark. Close-up through the windscreen, of RICCI, hugging BRUNO. Close-up of MANICONI at the wheel. Drops of rain begin to hit the windscreen.

MANICONI *while driving*: Another storm . . . *He starts the windscreen wipers* . . . It's ridiculous . . . there's nothing to do on Sundays . . . it always rains. I finish at one and then have to shut myself up at home. You just can't go out. *Quick cut to* RICCI *and* BRUNO. What can you do in this weather? Go to the cinema? That means nothing to me, absolutely nothing.

Seen through the windscreen, a pedestrian with an umbrella flashes across the road in front of the lorry. It is a near miss. BRUNO and RICCI react as the lorry swerves.

MANICONI *furious, sticks his head out the window*: Idiot! You blind . . . Eh . . . I should have run him over.

PEDESTRIAN *off*: Swine . . . Maniac . . .

MANICONI: Oh . . . learn to walk . . . piss off, you worm . . . *To* RICCI . . . They just fall under the wheels, these fools . . . And you end up in prison just like that . . . They sneak up, you don't see them, and splattt.

The lorry rolls on, the rain now torrential. From behind

49

the passengers, the windscreen is like a river, visibility almost zero.

MANICONI : Look at that, will you . . . Nice weather all week . . . and it pours on Sunday.

Long shot as the lorry advances through the deluge and then comes to a halt. RICCI *and* BRUNO *climb out, soaked within seconds, and hurry towards the stalls of the Porta Portese market. People are running for cover from the storm. In the background, the lorry drives off. Different long shots of the chaos caused by the rain in the market. The vendors pile their wares into carts. A disordered mass exodus crosses* RICCI'S *path. Father and son can be seen in the middle of the tumult,* RICCI *looking all around. Cut to a medium close-up of* RICCI, *looking helpless, his face wet and glistening. He glances down at* BRUNO. *Pan with the glance to* BRUNO, *his coat pulled up over his head. (Still on page 57) The music swells dramatically.* BRUNO, *sensing his father's attention, looks up at him.* RICCI *continues walking. A group of about twenty cyclists ride by, heading towards the road. One of them is also pushing a riderless bike along. Another is running and pushing a bike. Some others are riding their bikes with no hands and carrying another bike on their shoulders. Some young men take some bicycles, which are leaning against a wall, carry them hurriedly across the piazza, and pile them up on a waiting cart. A rapidly moving cart collides with another.* RICCI *and* BRUNO, *not knowing where to look or what to do, are despondent. Everything is falling apart and vanishing before their eyes.* RICCI *sees in the distance, the wall of a house which could provide some shelter. He signals* BRUNO *to follow and runs to the wall.* BRUNO *follows, trips and falls onto the flooded pavement, without his father noticing. (Still on page 58)* BRUNO *picks himself up and joins* RICCI *at the wall. Medium shot of* RICCI

*as he takes off his drooping hat and shakes the water
from it. He wipes his face with a handkerchief. As
BRUNO tries to dust the mud and water from his clothes,
RICCI notices the damage inflicted by the fall.*

RICCI *angrily* : What did you do to yourself? (*Still on page
58*)

BRUNO *defending himself* : I fell down.

RICCI *cooling down and handing him the handkerchief:* Here,
dry yourself off . . .

> *Medium close-up of* BRUNO *cleaning his legs with the
> handkerchief, then handing it back to his father. Pan
> with the handkerchief onto* RICCI *who wipes his face
> again while keeping an eye on the piazza. Long shot of
> the activity in the piazza. A man pushes a cart away
> from a cluster of stationary, seemingly abandoned, carts.
> While pushing the cart the man covers it with a water-
> proof sheet.*

MAN *to a colleague* : Hello, Righetto!

RIGHETTO : What's the matter? You afraid of the moths?

MAN : I don't like bathing with my clothes on.

> *So saying, he disappears with the cart. Return on* RICCI
> *still watching him. Close-up of* BRUNO *looking up at his
> father. Long shot of the piazza. Some men are trying to
> repair the canvas roof of one of the few remaining stalls.
> Close-up of* RICCI, *his depression mounting. Pan with a
> group of Austrian priests, cackling in German, who run
> towards the wall and shelter themselves on either side of*
> RICCI *and* BRUNO. *Once safe from the rain their chatter
> becomes indistinguishable. They snigger at their own
> remarks. Close-up of* BRUNO *squashed between a cassock
> and his father. Close-up of* RICCI *listening to the remarks
> without understanding. A young priest smiles at* BRUNO
> *who returns a less than friendly glance. Medium close-up
> of* RICCI, *as the rain is diminishing and a ray of sunlight
> appears. As the sun breaks through, the priests continue
> their tour of the market. Suddenly* RICCI'S *gaze is*

*fastened on something or somebody in the piazza. He
takes a step forward. Long shot of the piazza, a young
cyclist, with hair and clothes like the* THIEF, *rides quickly
up to an* OLD MAN, *and stops in front of him. He gives
the* OLD MAN *a bank note from his pocket. Medium
close-up of the two.*

OLD MAN : What's this? Only a hundred lire!

THIEF : That'll have to do for today . . . Bye . . .

OLD MAN : And what use is this? What use is it?

THIEF *leaving* : Good-bye!

Medium shot of RICCI. *Pan, then lateral track with him
as he tears off towards the* THIEF *with* BRUNO *following.*

RICCI : Stop him! Stop him! Thief . . . thief . . .

Long shot of RICCI *running and shouting. His cries
are almost entirely muffled by the noise of the renewed
activity in the market. Long shot of an open space at the
edge of the market, the* THIEF *accelerating fast in the
distance.* RICCI *keeps after him, but soon realises the
futility of the chase. He stops and retraces his steps,*
BRUNO *still following.*

RICCI : Hurry, Bruno . . . We've got to catch that old man.

They run towards the camera. BRUNO *suddenly points
excitedly.*

BRUNO : There he is, papa . . . There . . .

In long shot, the OLD MAN *is seen, about to disappear
round the corner of the street.* BRUNO *and* RICCI *chase
after him. At first* RICCI *pulls the boy along by the hand,
but he soon lets go so that he can run faster.* BRUNO
follows, jumping the occasional puddle. The OLD MAN
*has turned the corner into a tiny street which leads into
a piazza hidden between some houses.* RICCI *and* BRUNO
arrive, running, in the piazza. The OLD MAN *is not there.
They turn and run back to the street.* RICCI *runs into a
half-open door,* BRUNO *arrives just behind him. The hall,
seen from their point of view, is empty.* BRUNO *abruptly
shoots off down the street.*

RICCI : Where's that bastard gone? . . . Bruno, where are you going?

Pan with BRUNO'S *zig-zag path. As* RICCI *enters shot,* BRUNO *appears at the end of the next street. He stops and signals that he has found nothing. Then, like a rabbit, bounds down another street.* RICCI *continues his own search in a street leading off the square. He looks into another doorway, but it, too, is empty.* RICCI *looks all around, then goes into a yet unexplored street, either to find his son or the* OLD MAN.
In long shot, at the end of a long alley-way, the OLD MAN *appears, carrying some tin pails. With a shuffling gait, he moves away.* RICCI *runs to the end of the street and calls out. No one answers; there is nothing to be seen. In the distance, behind* RICCI, *is the street which* BRUNO *had earlier dashed down, and from which he now reappears, disappointed by his failure to find anything. After a short look round, he starts to unbutton his pants, moving all the time towards the nearest wall. Just as he reaches the wall and is about to start urinating, his father arrives in shot.*

RICCI : Bruno . . . Quickly! He's over there!

BRUNO, *startled by his father's arrival, turns towards his father and runs after him without having time to urinate. Lateral track in medium shot on* RICCI, *who is walking with increasing speed, towards the* OLD MAN. *While buttoning up his trousers,* BRUNO *follows him, running, then walking. Medium close-up of the* OLD MAN, *behind him.* RICCI *and* BRUNO *are catching up. Lateral track as* RICCI *and* BRUNO *get to a bridge just behind the* OLD MAN. *Medium close-up of them.*

RICCI : Excuse me, I want to talk to you. That young man who was with you . . . I want to see him. Where can I find him?

OLD MAN : What young man?

RICCI : The one you were talking to . . . on the bicycle.

OLD MAN: Why? What's he done to you?

RICCI: Nothing . . . I just want to talk to him about a personal matter . . . It's very urgent.

OLD MAN: What do you want me to tell you? I don't know anything. I don't know him.

RICCI *insistently*: But this young man . . . he was with you . . . near the arcade . . . at Porta Portese . . .

OLD MAN: Ah! You want some of the young boys who wait in the arcades, huh? *The end of this sentence is spoken off, with close-up on* BRUNO, *listening.*

RICCI *off*: Hey . . . Come here . . . Listen . . .

Cut to medium close-up of RICCI, *grabbing the* OLD MAN *by the collar.*

RICCI: I must find him . . . You must tell me where he is!

OLD MAN *extricating himself*: Look here . . . Stop it! Who do you think you are, anyway?

BRUNO *takes hold of the* OLD MAN'S *coat who again pulls himself free.* (*Still on page 59*)

OLD MAN *to* BRUNO: Let me go, little brat. You should be ashamed of yourself . . . pushing round an old man . . . on his last legs. Terrible . . . terrible . . . what a world!

Pan with him as he moves away across the bridge. Gradually he breaks into a run.

Long shot of a small piazza. In the background, an architecturally undistinguished church and another building which might be an alms-house or a presbytery. RICCI *and* BRUNO *enter shot in the foreground, backs to camera, running, and stopping in front of the church. Medium shot of a door near the church's porch, where men and women, the majority in tattered clothes, are going in, pushing each other.* RICCI *and* BRUNO *approach.*

Cut to the door from inside the church as the people enter. RICCI, *rather surprised, waits for a moment in the door,* BRUNO *beside him. Long shot of the packed hallway with its high vaulted ceiling. Religious organ music and the chant of prayers. A dignified man in a white smock is giving an old man a shave, while others line up for their turn. A gaudily dressed woman in a large hat moves among the poor, directing them to the chapel entrance, her expression more haughty than benevolent. She comes towards the* OLD MAN, *with whom* RICCI *has once again caught up. The* OLD MAN *takes his hat off as the* LADY *approaches.*

LADY *to the* OLD MAN : You're late, my friend . . . You should have been here at ten.

An elegant young man passes across frame, jostling everyone in his path.

YOUNG MAN : Hurry up . . . Move along . . . Don't dawdle.

OLD MAN *to* LADY : I'm sorry . . . I didn't know . . . They told me it was always open.

RICCI *follows a woman with a scruffy baby through the door. Crane up and back, as* RICCI *and* BRUNO *make their way through the crowd of poor people and ' good people ', who administer to the needs of the poor.* RICCI *catches a glimpse of the* OLD MAN *who is smoothing his hair while talking to the* LADY. *The man in the white smock is cutting someone's hair not far from* RICCI.

OLD MAN *to the* LADY : Can I have my dinner?

LADY : After the Mass . . . Put your bowl down . . . *To every-one* . . . Those of you who are here for the first time, I must tell you to leave your bowls in the courtyard.

The LADY *turns and directs the people to the chapel entrance. The* OLD MAN *walks away from the main line of people, and goes out a different door.* RICCI *and* BRUNO *dash to a window to see where the* OLD MAN *is going.*

Long shot of the courtyard with a long trestle-table in the centre. Behind the table, near some huge cooking pots, a handful of serving girls busy with their preparations; and on the table, the bowls for the poor are laid out. The OLD MAN *goes towards one of the girls.*

GIRL : Line them up neatly . . . one next to the other. We must have some order . . . not like the last time. Everyone'll

55

have his own mug and bowl.

> *The* OLD MAN *puts his bowl on the table, and walks back towards the church.*
>
> RICCI, *in the hallway, moves purposefully towards the* OLD MAN, *but he is stopped by the* YOUNG MAN.

YOUNG MAN : Do you want a shave?

RICCI : No.

YOUNG MAN : Well, then, go to the Mass.

> *The* YOUNG MAN *leads the way, but* RICCI *goes after the* OLD MAN *instead. One of the ' barbers ' is about to shave the* OLD MAN.

MAN *to the* OLD MAN : There you are . . . sit down.

> *He helps him to sit, and fastens a white towel around his neck. Medium shot of* RICCI, *with* BRUNO *at his side, staring resolutely at the* OLD MAN *who is out of shot. Long shot of the hallway, the* LADY, *still frantically active, passes by* RICCI *and* BRUNO *as she moves towards the ' barber '.*

LADY : Hurry up . . . into the church . . . come along . . . come along . . .

> *Medium close-up of the* LADY; *the ' barber ' who is lathering the* OLD MAN'S *face, and in the background,* RICCI *and* BRUNO.

LADY *to the ' barber '* : Tell me, Reverend, will you be much longer?

REVEREND : No . . . I have nearly finished . . . I just have this one . . . and . . . oh . . . him . . . *Pointing to* RICCI.

RICCI : No . . . no . . . me, no.

LADY : Then . . . if you can hurry up . . . the Mass is about to start.

REVEREND : Yes . . . yes . . .

> *She moves away. Medium shot of the* REVEREND *continuing to lather the face of the* OLD MAN, *who is anxiously keeping an eye on* RICCI. RICCI *still staring. Close-up of* OLD MAN *trying to out-stare* RICCI, *but he eventually looks down. Medium close-up on* BRUNO, *taut-faced,*

*almost adult, staring with chin resting in his hand. Very
big close-up of the razor moving down the* OLD MAN'S
cheek.

OLD MAN : If you don't mind sir, don't shave my chin . . .
I want to grow a goatee . . . just do the other side and that'll
be enough.

LADY *off* : Hurry up . . . hurry. *In long shot.* Reverend, the
priest is waiting. You can do the rest later.

She turns, sees BRUNO, *and takes him by the hand.*

LADY : Come on, boy, come along with me.

BRUNO *manages to escape and rejoin his father, just as
the* OLD MAN *is leaving the barber's chair. He follows
in the* LADY'S *footsteps.*

REVEREND *trying to get his smock off* : Will someone please
help me . . . I can't do it by myself.

RICCI *and* BRUNO *follow the* OLD MAN *to the church
entrance.*

*Long shot of the church, very full. The organ echoes the
' Ave Maria '. Some of the poor people piously take their
seats, others remain standing.* RICCI *and* BRUNO *are in the
back of the church. Pan with them as they work their way
through the crowd until they reach an imposing column.
In the background, the officiating priest moves down the
main aisle surrounded by choir boys. Medium shot of
the front rows reserved for the charitable ladies, some
of whom take their places while continuing to keep a
maternal eye on the flock. Medium shot of the* OLD MAN
*seated uncomfortably between two others. He is watching
someone. Medium shot of* RICCI, *next to the column, as
he catches sight of the* OLD MAN. *He immediately signals
to* BRUNO *to remain where he is. Lateral track with* RICCI
as he moves down one of the rows, arrives behind the
OLD MAN, *and, with some difficulty, squeezes himself
down the row next to him.*

RICCI *to the person next to him* : Slide along a little !

RICCI *manages to sit down. Medium close-up of the two.*

RICCI *looks at him, but the* OLD MAN *directs his eyes to the altar, out of shot. Medium shot of the ladies who are distributing books of prayers and songs. (Still on page 60) Pan with them, then back to a medium close-up of* RICCI *and the* OLD MAN.

RICCI *whispering*: That young bloke . . . I must find him . . . I've got to speak to him . . . Can you tell me where he is?

Behind them the ladies are distributing the books.

OLD MAN *whispering*: But what do you want me to say? This bloke . . . that one . . . another. I don't know. I don't know anything.

Long shot of the church from behind the altar. In the foreground the communion rail. Near it a prayer-stool at which the REVEREND *kneels, opens a missal, and turns to the poor.*

REVEREND: Page six.

He puts on his glasses and begins to read a prayer. Each of his phrases is repeated in litany by the faithful poor.

REVEREND: I want to leave this holy place with a pure soul and a peace of mind. I try again to overcome the weakness of my flesh . . .

The prayer continues off, and becomes indistinguishable in the background as the camera tracks along the rows of people and comes to a halt on RICCI *and the* OLD MAN.

RICCI: It's for his own good, this business. Where is he?

OLD MAN: I'm no informer. Leave me in peace.

RICCI: You know him . . . If you don't tell me, I'll call the police.

OLD MAN: I never did anything to you . . . Leave me alone!

RICCI: Tell me where he is . . . that's all I need to know . . . You've nothing to lose . . . nothing at all . . . I have nothing against you . . . I'll even give you something.

RICCI *takes out his wallet as the* OLD MAN *watches him. The* LADY *passes behind them and hands each of them a meal voucher.*

OLD MAN *to* LADY : What are we eating?

LADY : Pasta and potatoes.

She moves out of shot. Track into close-up of RICCI.

RICCI : Well, are you going to tell me? Yes or no? If I take you to the police, it won't be easy to wriggle out of. Where is he?

OLD MAN : Oh . . . try Via Campanelle . . .

RICCI : What number?

OLD MAN : I don't know . . . fifteen . . . or perhaps it's twenty.

RICCI : You can come with me, then . . .

OLD MAN *aghast* : Me?

RICCI : Yes, you . . .

LADY : Shhh . . . If you don't keep quiet, I'll send you out.

Long shot, from high angle, of the church. The LADY *walks away from* RICCI *and the* OLD MAN *towards the back of the church. The people have started a chant that continues until the end of the scene. Medium close-up of* RICCI *and the* OLD MAN *as* RICCI *tries to drag the* OLD MAN *out.*

RICCI : Are you coming or not? You've nothing to lose.

OLD MAN : Go by yourself . . . I'm staying here.

RICCI : If I lose my temper . . .

OLD MAN : Will you shut up and let me be?

RICCI : All right . . . the police . . . you'll see . . .

OLD MAN : Go on . . . get them . . . just leave me alone . . .

RICCI *pinning the* OLD MAN *down brutally* : That's enough . . . Come on . . .

LADY *turning* : Shush!

RICCI pushing and pulling the OLD MAN *out.*

RICCI : You stubborn fool . . . you're coming with me . . .

OLD MAN : But where? You're lucky I'm a feeble old man otherwise you'd have a fist in the face . . .

RICCI : Look . . . I've had enough . . . understand?

Medium shot of the LADY *and the* YOUNG MAN. *Camera tracks back with them as they come to see what all the fuss is about.* RICCI *in close-up dragging at the* OLD MAN.

63

OLD MAN : Big as you are . . . it's not you who's going to take me where I don't want to go . . .

RICCI : Move!

Pan with them up to the column. The OLD MAN *stops.*

OLD MAN : At least let me have some food.

RICCI : Yes . . . all right . . . but I'm coming with you.

OLD MAN : For once I could have had a peaceful meal!

Medium shot of the LADY *and the* YOUNG MAN *who have discovered the source of the trouble.*

LADY *to* YOUNG MAN : Go on.

Just as RICCI *and the* OLD MAN *are about to go out into the courtyard.*

YOUNG MAN : Hey . . . you can't leave . . . it's not allowed.

OLD MAN : I'm going to eat.

RICCI : And I'm going with him.

YOUNG MAN : No . . . no . . . after the Mass . . . after. You can't go now. Shhhh . . .

The bell for the Elevation of the Host rings. Everyone kneels down piously, except the OLD MAN *who takes this opportunity to escape.* RICCI *and* BRUNO *take off after him.*

Long shot of an empty corridor. In the distance RICCI *and his son are walking quickly towards camera.*

Long shot of the courtyard. RICCI *and* BRUNO, *back to camera, walk towards one of the serving girls.*

RICCI : Hey, Miss . . . did anyone come out here?

GIRL : No . . . no one . . . besides it's not time yet.

RICCI *turns and retraces his steps.* BRUNO *hesitates for a moment then follows.*

In the corridor, RICCI *and* BRUNO *try to get out through the door at the end, but it is locked. The* YOUNG MAN, *furiously, enters shot. Medium shot of him.*

YOUNG MAN : Would you mind telling me what you are doing here?

RICCI : I want to get out.

YOUNG MAN : You can't go through this way. It's shut. The

Reverend has forbidden it. So please stop all this din. This is a church!

> RICCI *and* BRUNO *rush towards the door which leads into the church.*
>
> *Medium shot of* RICCI *inside the church. He edges through the people.* BRUNO, *having trouble keeping up, finally stops. Pan in to a slightly tilted-down long shot on* RICCI, *who reaches the entrance to the church. The* YOUNG MAN *still chasing him.*

YOUNG MAN: Did you come here with the intention of causing trouble? What do you want, anyway?

RICCI : I must find him. He must still be here.

> *Close-up of* BRUNO *who is looking around for the* OLD MAN. *Suddenly he has an idea. He hurries towards the confessional and pulls the central curtain aside. Medium close-up of an aged priest, who angrily raises his hand. Close-up of* BRUNO, *as the priest's hand strikes the boy's head.* BRUNO *then turns and makes his way towards his father, who is still being chased.* RICCI *crosses the central aisle. His pursuers stop, genuflect, and make the sign of the cross. Medium shot of* RICCI, *near the door leading to the sacristy.*

YOUNG MAN : What are you doing there?

RICCI : I'm looking for the old man who was here. I must find him.

ANOTHER YOUNG MAN : Well, find him after the Mass. This is just too much.

> *Camera tracks in behind* RICCI *going into the sacristy, where every available surface is covered with vestments and curtains, and filled with statues. The two* YOUNG MEN *follow him in, as does* BRUNO.

RICCI : He must be in here.

YOUNG MEN : Shhhh.

> RICCI *lifts a tapestry and discovers an open window.*

RICCI : This is where he got out.

YOUNG MAN : Will you get out? Now!

Bruno *and* Ricci *head towards a little door and go out. Cut to* Bruno *and* Ricci, *running through an open space next to the church.*

Bruno: God knows where he's gone now!

Ricci *stopping*: Oh, be quiet . . . He couldn't have flown away.

Long shot of the open field. Medium close-up of Bruno *slightly from above, as if seen by his father.*

Bruno: I wouldn't have let him go for the food . . .

Ricci *in medium close-up, slightly from below*: Oh . . shut up, will you!

Ricci *raises his hand. Medium close-up of* Bruno, *receiving a blow. Silence.* Bruno *looks at his father.* Ricci *looks penitently at* Bruno, *but is unable to say anything. Medium shot of* Bruno *crying, and trying to escape his father's grasp.* Bruno *runs away.* Ricci *takes a few steps after him.*

Bruno *sobbing*: Leave me alone!

Ricci: Where are you going?

Bruno: Back to the house . . .

Ricci: Bruno, come over here . . .

Bruno: No . . . you hit me . . .

Ricci: Come here at once.

Bruno: No!

Ricci: Come here or I'll come and get you.

Bruno: No . . . I'm going.

Ricci *shouting*: Bruno!

Medium shot of Bruno *half-hidden behind a tree;* Ricci *standing about twenty feet away looking at him.*

Ricci: Bruno . . . you're going to do as I say . . . do you understand . . . you impudent brat . . . come here . . .

Bruno: No . . . I won't . . . Why did you hit me?

Ricci: Because you were getting on my nerves. Now come along with me.

Bruno: No . . . go by yourself.

Ricci *in close-up, furious*: Bruno, you're going to obey me!

Medium shot of BRUNO. *Sobbing, he looks down, sulking with his hands in his trouser pockets, and walks slowly towards his father.*

RICCI *off*: Get going, you little trouble-maker . . .

BRUNO *comes over next to his father. Camera tracks back with them walking.*

BRUNO *muttering*: You're horrible . . .

RICCI: Enough . . . shut up . . . little brat . . .

BRUNO: I'm going to tell mother . . . you'll see . . .

RICCI: Wait until we get home!

Long shot of a wide avenue and a bridge which crosses the Tiber. BRUNO *and* RICCI *walking together, but apart.*

RICCI: Go and wait for me on the bridge . . . and don't budge. . . . I'm going to look for the old man.

BRUNO *does as he is told, and moves slowly towards the bridge. Dissolve.*

Long shot of RICCI *moving down towards the banks of the river. Medium shot of* BRUNO *brooding, immobile in the sun, an occasional tear sliding down his cheeks.* RICCI *walking along, looking around. Pan along the embankment.* RICCI *is suddenly surprised by distant cries.*

VOICE: Help! Help!

RICCI, *concerned, looks towards the bridge. (Still on page 60)*

VOICES *off*: Over there . . . Someone drowning . . . Where? See . . . get help . . . he's fallen in . . . Get a boat . . . By the arch there . . . Hurry . . .

RICCI, *now frightened, runs towards the foot of the bridge. Camera tracks with him.*

RICCI *crying*: Bruno . . . Bruno . . .

VOICES: Hurry . . . over there . . .

Long shot of RICCI, *back to camera, running frantically towards the bridge. His voice echoes as he runs under an arch.*

RICCI: Bruno . . . Bruno . . .

Long shot of the other side of the bridge. Near one of

the supports in the middle of the river is a small boat, dragging a body. (Still on page 77) Some men wade out into the river to bring it ashore. Others wait anxiously on the shore. In the foreground, with back to camera, RICCI watches. The boat arrives at the bank. Close-up of RICCI, shattered.

RICCI *murmuring*: Bruno . . .

VOICES : Gently . . . put him down on the grass.
Long shot of the body being carried (Still on page 77) and stretched out on the ground.

VOICES : Careful of his head . . . give him some air . . .
The body seems too large to be a child's. RICCI, stunned, turns to look up to the top of the bridge. Long shot of the long stone stairway leading up to the bridge. BRUNO is sitting on the top step.

VOICES *off*: Not dead . . . is he? . . . No . . . he's all right . . .
Cut to medium shot of BRUNO, pulling off his jacket, and looking down towards the crowd. Close-up of RICCI very relieved. RICCI, with back to camera, taking the steps four at a time, leaps up to his son. Medium shot of BRUNO at the top of the steps, he has got to his feet and takes a few tentative steps. His father, short of breath, comes up to him, and picks up his jacket.

RICCI : Put your jacket back on, Bruno . . . you'll catch cold . . .
They walk side by side across the bridge. RICCI tries to help BRUNO put the jacket on, but BRUNO insists on doing it without any paternal help. In the background, a small group of people look over the side of the bridge at the rescue operation.
Medium shot of a treelined avenue, running along the Tiber. Camera tracks back with them. BRUNO is dragging his feet. RICCI eventually stops walking.

RICCI : You tired?
BRUNO looks down and nods his head, feebly. Then he looks over to a large stone block.

Ricci : Sit down there . . . There's nothing else to do . . . We should go home . . .

Bruno sits on the stone as his father leans against the nearby wall. The shouts of a passing group cause them to look around.

Voices : Viva Modena ! Viva Modena !

Long shot of the avenue. Pan with a lorry as it passes them. In the lorry, a crowd of young people are singing and shouting enthusiastically. A large sign which reads: FORZA MODENA.

Cut back to Ricci in medium close-up.

Ricci : Is Modena a good team?

Medium close-up of Bruno, a little less unhappy, but still unreceptive, shaking his head distastefully. Cut back to Ricci.

Ricci : Are you hungry?

Cut back to Bruno from his father's point of view. He looks up sharply and nods emphatically. Ricci takes out his wallet, and counts his money. Bruno watches his father's hands. Medium close-up of Ricci.

Ricci : Could you manage a pizza?

Bruno's face lights up in assent. Cut back to Ricci straightening up, and indicating with a look to the other side of the avenue.

Ricci : Come on then . . . they must have them there.

High angle in long shot, as Bruno gets up. Ricci takes his arm.

Ricci : Let's go . . . When it's finished, it's finished . . . no point in standing around here.

They cross the avenue. Fade to black.

Cut to long shot inside the café facing the entrance. On a small platform, near the door, a café orchestra: violin, bass, guitar, and a singer, accompanying himself on a guitar. In the foreground, a few customers. As father and son enter, Ricci seems surprised by the elegance of the surroundings. Long shot of the room from Ricci's

*position. It is, in fact, quite full. The waiters move
amongst the tables. It is very noisy.* RICCI *hesitates, looks
at* BRUNO, *and decides to fulfil his promise.*

RICCI: Over here, Bruno.

*Pan with them as they find a table and sit down facing
each other.*

RICCI: Sit there . . .

RICCI *takes off his hat;* BRUNO *his scarf. In the background, the waiters go about their business. Medium
close-up of the two of them at the table.*

RICCI: Now don't worry about anything . . . We're going to
have a good feed . . .

Close-up of BRUNO, *silent, proud, and very happy.
Medium close-up of* RICCI *gesturing to a waiter.*

RICCI: Waiter!

Long shot of the room. A waiter turns to look at RICCI.
*Then with obvious disdain calls to a colleague and con-
tinues taking another order.*

WAITER: Arrigo, take care of that gentleman will you . . .

*Another waiter moves towards camera. Camera tracks
back and pans to frame* RICCI *and* BRUNO *at the table.
The waiter, back to camera, wipes the table.*

ARRIGO: Half a bottle?

RICCI: No, a whole bottle and two pizzas.

ARRIGO *haughtily*: We don't do pizzas here . . .

Close-up of BRUNO.

RICCI *off*: What? You don't do pizzas . . .

ARRIGO *off*: This is a restaurant, not a pizzeria.

General shot of the three.

RICCI: Well, then, we'll have a meal.

ARRIGO: A meal?

RICCI: What do you have?

Close-up of BRUNO *turning and looking enviously at the
neighbouring table.*

ARRIGO *off, impatiently*: What do you want?

The next table, from BRUNO'S *viewpoint. A middle-class*

family on a Sunday outing. A girl, about BRUNO'S *age, turns towards him. Close-up of* RICCI, *who is also looking at the next table.*

RICCI : Would you like a mozzarella in carrozzo, too?

BRUNO *excited* : Oh, yes . . . yes, please.

RICCI : Waiter, two mozzarellas and wine, immediately!

The WAITER *bows and moves off.* RICCI *leans forward towards his son.*

RICCI : Now, we'll eat and after I'll get you a cake as well. . . . You happy?

Close-up of BRUNO, *nodding; his eyes shining with joy.* BRUNO *glances at the next table again. Cut to the girl who looks away snobbishly.* BRUNO, *looking with admiration at his father. Medium close-up of* RICCI *leaning back happily in his chair, his hand tapping out the rhythm of the orchestra's music, on the table. Reverse shot of* BRUNO, *smiling. The* WAITER *puts a cover on the table, then two glasses and a carafe of wine. After a pause,* RICCI *takes the carafe and fills both glasses.* BRUNO *looks in amazement at his wine-filled glass.*

RICCI *drinks his glass down in one gulp, sighs and looks at his son.*

RICCI : Don't you want to drink yours?

Close-up of BRUNO *who awkwardly takes two sips.* RICCI *laughs.*

RICCI : If your mother only knew I was letting you drink!

Close-up of BRUNO *putting down his glass and smiling.*

RICCI : Well, mustn't worry about it . . .

RICCI *looks at the orchestra. Track in to the singer whose expression changes with every chord. Intercut shots of* BRUNO *laughing, his father smiling, the singer, and then the other musicians who are shouting ' olé! olé! '. Long shot of the room, the* WAITER *arrives with a plate in each hand and places them before* RICCI *and* BRUNO. *The boy looks at his plate with delight, takes a serviette, and a knife and fork. With obvious difficulty, he tries to cut*

71

his food. RICCI *is having no trouble at all.*

RICCI: Eat up . . .

BRUNO *still in trouble.* RICCI *goes on eating.*

RICCI: Everything sorts itself out, except death.

BRUNO, *discouraged, drops his knife and fork, and eats the mozzarella with his fingers. (Still on page 78) He amuses himself with the long strands of melted cheese which connect the cheese in his mouth with that in his hand. He sneaks a look at the girl who is eating with great propriety. Shot of* RICCI *eating enthusiastically and pouring himself another glass. The next table, from* RICCI'S *point of view, as the* WAITER *brings them some cakes and a bottle of champagne. Medium shot of* BRUNO *also watching, astonished by the number of delicacies. The little girl makes a face at* BRUNO *while devouring a cake. Close-up of* RICCI, *his expression serious.*

RICCI: To pay for a meal like that, you'd have to earn . . . *Close-up of* BRUNO . . . *off* . . . I don't know . . . about a million a month . . .

On hearing the amount, BRUNO *drops his food into his plate and stares, horrified, at his father. Shot of* RICCI, *seeing his son's reaction.*

RICCI: Come on . . . eat . . . don't think about it . . .

BRUNO *picks up his food and continues eating.*

RICCI *off*: Is it good?

BRUNO *nods.* RICCI *stops eating, and dreamily pushes his plate to one side.*

RICCI: And to think . . . Everything was going to be all right . . . I'd worked it out . . . With the extras that we would make . . . *He takes a pencil out and starts to write on the paper serviette* . . . let's see . . . yes . . . twelve thousand . . . basic . . . and . . . *Handing the paper and pencil to* BRUNO . . . Here . . . you do it.

Close-up of BRUNO *who takes the paper and begins to write. With his left hand he holds the cheese which he continues to nibble.*

72

RICCI *off*: . . . 12,000 basic, 2,000 overtime, plus family allowances 800 a day . . . 800 by 30 . . . what does that come to?

After adding it up, BRUNO *shows his father the total.* RICCI *reads it.*

RICCI: . . . What more could you want? . . . I could never have earned that much before . . . And today I'm supposed to give it all up! . . . No, I won't . . . never. We must find that bicycle . . . without it we can't eat . . . What can you do?

BRUNO: We'll have to go to Porta Portese every day. We've got to find those people!

RICCI: Yes . . . but they'll never show themselves there now. We won't find it, even though your mother lit a candle . . . We won't find it, even with the aid of the Saints.

His face is lit up as an idea strikes him. Track in and dissolve.

Camera cuts to RICCI *and* BRUNO, *walking down a sunny little street. As they move along the pavement, their steps quicken.* RICCI *stops before* SIGNORA SANTONA'S *apartment building. As they climb the stairs, they hear a radio.*

RADIO: . . . and now for the sports news. Today being Sunday, there are a large number of matches up and down the country. The line-up of teams is . . .

Low shot of RICCI *and* BRUNO *as they reach the door of* SIGNORA SANTONA'S *apartment.*

RADIO: . . . Lazio versus Fiorentina in Florence, Rome versus Modena in Rome . . .

Inside the apartment, RICCI *and* BRUNO *move down the corridor. The same* WOMAN *is in the kitchen making tea.*

WOMAN *without turning*: Last door at the end . . .

Lateral track with the two. RICCI *takes off his hat, as they arrive at the door behind an elderly lady, a young woman and a woman on crutches. Medium shot of this group.*

73

GRANDMOTHER : I'm afraid of what she'll say . . .

OTHER WOMAN : You mustn't be afraid, Maria, tell her everything . . . Then, you'll see . . . she'll cure you . . .

GRANDMOTHER : Praise be to God . . . Oh . . . Blessed Virgin!

Pan with them as they go into the fortune-teller's room. Long shot of the room, full of clients. SIGNORA SANTONA *is seated, still in her dressing gown.*

ASSISTANT *pointing* : This one, yes . . . That one, no.

Track in on RICCI *who is standing near* BRUNO *at the door.*

SIGNORA SANTONA : You must sew your seed in another field, my son. Do you understand?

The WOMAN *from the kitchen passes* RICCI, *carrying a tray of tea things. Pan with her as she moves behind* SIGNORA SANTONA *who is still talking to a loudly-dressed man of about thirty. Behind the man, an older woman, probably his mother.*

MAN : No, I don't understand.

SIGNORA SANTONA : But how can you not . . . it's simple. What is the point of digging and furrowing in a barren field? You sow, but do not reap. *Close-up of the* MAN, *shocked. Off.* Do you understand now?

MAN : No, not really.

SIGNORA SANTONA *in medium shot* : The woman does not love you. You must forget her . . . *Cut to him, upset* . . . and you're ugly, my boy, but there are plenty of women in the world . . . Sow your seed elsewhere . . . Well?

Medium close-up of the MAN *who, while nodding approvingly, takes out his wallet.* SIGNORA SANTONA'S ASSISTANT *leans forward and hands her the tea.*

ASSISTANT : It's getting cold, mother.

SIGNORA SANTONA *to the* MAN : Good-bye . . .

The MAN *hands a banknote to another assistant, and walks out.*

MAN : Thank you and good-bye.

As he goes out of the door with his mother, BRUNO *leaps*

up and signals to his father.

BRUNO : Over here, papa . . . here's a seat free.

BRUNO *takes up his position in front of the chair just vacated by the* MAN.

CLIENT : Listen, boy . . . get back.

Pan with RICCI *as he crosses to the chair* BRUNO *is guarding. The other clients gesticulate and complain.*

OLD LADY : Now, little one . . .wait your turn.

ANOTHER LADY : Everyone must wait their turn. You must respect that. That's fair, isn't it? There are people who have been standing waiting for two hours. Myself, for example.

MAN : But I was here long before you, little boy. Papa! papa! . . . Papa nothing. We should . . .

RICCI *upset* : I'm in rather a hurry, though.

MAN : So am I in a hurry.

WOMAN : You've got some cheek . . . I've been waiting for over an hour.

RICCI : But I really am in a great hurry.

WOMAN : But we all are.

RICCI : Please be kind enough to let me go first.

ANOTHER WOMAN : It's extraordinary. There are always people who want to be first.

Medium shot of SIGNORA SANTONA, *sipping her tea indifferently.*

SIGNORA SANTONA : Come on, now . . . my friends . . . don't fight.

WOMAN *off* : All the same, it's completely unfair. We have other things to do too, you know.

High angle long shot of the discussion as they jerk about like puppets.

Cut back to SIGNORA SANTONA, *folding her hands.*

SIGNORA SANTONA : Now . . . now . . . You'll have your turn, all of you.

Behind her, the ASSISTANT *points.*

ASSISTANT : This one, yes . . . *To* RICCI . . . That one, no.

SIGNORA SANTONA *raising her hands skywards* : O Lord . . .

Give me the light . . . Give me the light.

Medium shot of SANTONA *facing* RICCI.

SIGNORA SANTONA : What do you want, my son?

RICCI : Some one stole . . .

SIGNORA SANTONA : What did they steal?

RICCI : My bicycle!

SIGNORA SANTONA : Your bicycle . . . What do you want me to tell you, my son? . . . I can't see what I can tell you . . . I can only tell you what I see . . . Listen . . . either you will find it immediately or you will never find it . . . Understand?

RICCI : Immediately? But where do I look?

SIGNORA SANTONA : I can tell you no more. Go and try to understand. Either you will find it immediately or you will never find it. (*Still on page 78*)

> *Dissatisfied,* RICCI *digs into his pocket, while* SIGNORA SANTONA *with feigned discretion examines her fingernails.* RICCI *and* BRUNO *study the wallet's contents.* BRUNO *takes a small note out and hands it to* SIGNORA SANTONA *who closes her eyes in shock.* RICCI *gets up from the chair. The* ASSISTANT *takes the money from* BRUNO. *Pan with* RICCI *and* BRUNO *as they leave the room.*

RICCI *dryly* : Thank you . . . Good-bye.

SIGNORA SANTONA : Good-bye, my son.

> *The father and son go out of the door.*

SIGNORA SANTONA *off* : Well, what have you to tell me today, Adele?

ADELE *off* : My husband gets drunk every day.

SIGNORA SANTONA *off* : Oh, my dear, what a cross to bear! Don't give him any money.

ADELE *off* : What am I to do? He just takes it . . .

> RICCI *and* BRUNO *walk slowly down the stairs towards the street.* RICCI *puts his hat back on.*
>
> *Cut to medium shot of* RICCI *and* BRUNO *leaving the building. They hesitate an instant in front of the door. A distant bell rings, probably for vespers. They start off slowly.*

Low angle, in another street, of Ricci *in medium close-up. They stop sharply and fix on something out of shot. Medium close-up of* Bruno, *up against his father's legs. He looks out of shot and then up to his father. Cut to a medium close-up of what they see on the other side of the road. It is the* Thief, *who turns and recognizes them. Cut to big close-up of* Ricci. *Cut back to big close-up of* Thief.

Long shot of the street. Ricci *and* Bruno *facing the* Thief, *who is standing about a dozen feet away from them. He affects a carefree gait, and tries to move by them while hugging the wall. Medium shot of him, as he continues walking and glancing back.* Ricci *and* Bruno *are right behind him, but at the crossroad the* Thief *dashes round the corner and disappears into the next street.* Ricci *and* Bruno *give chase.*

Another street. The Thief *runs in front of camera towards an arched 'portalinto' through which he disappears.* Ricci *follows him in, and, a few seconds later, so does* Bruno.

Inside the entrance hall Ricci *and* Bruno *find themselves in front of a wrought iron and glass door, art nouveau style. On the wall next to the door, the sign: ENTRANCE FORBIDDEN TO MINORS. In medium shot,* Ricci *knocks impatiently. A female silhouette arrives behind the door.*

Licensee *off*: It's closed. *He knocks again.* The young ladies are having lunch. *He knocks again, loudly. The woman half-opens the door.* When we're shut . . . we're shut for everyone. Understand?

She slams the door, but Ricci *stops it from closing. He pushes it open and runs past the* Licensee. Bruno *tries to follow his father.*

Licensee: Ah . . . look at this . . . What next? A child! A child! You! No, you don't . . . You're not coming in here. Get out . . . Get out . . . Now.

81

She manages to close the door. BRUNO *has not managed to enter. He stands in the entrance, puzzled.*

LICENSEE *screaming off*: You too . . . Get out! Didn't you hear . . . you can't come in. You can't come in here!

In long shot, slightly tilted up, RICCI *runs across the reception room of the brothel to some stairs.*

LICENSEE: Where do you think you're going now?

As he climbs the stairs, RICCI *passes a girl, half-dressed and surprised, on her way down. She walks off into an adjacent room, as the* LICENSEE *reaches the foot of the stairs.*

LICENSEE: It's not hours . . . you can't be here . . . you can't go upstairs . . . we're shut . . . now out . . . get out!

Cut back to BRUNO, *still waiting in the entranceway, he looks up at the sign on the wall.*

LICENSEE *off*: The law is the same for everyone. Do you understand?

BRUNO *walks pensively out to the street.*

VOICES *off*: Where is he? . . . Where did he go? There he is. Grab him!

Cut back to RICCI *as he resists the attempt of the* LICENSEE *and an older woman to push him towards the exit. Screams and shouts.*

LICENSEE: What a way to carry on . . . you swine!

RICCI: Let me go . . . I must talk to the man who came in here.

RICCI *breaks free, and makes for the door the girl went through earlier. Camera tracks with him entering the room at the same moment as he does.*

Long shot of the dining-room, its walls decorated with photos of actors and pin-ups. The prostitutes are seated, in various degrees of undress, around a large central table. RICCI *enters, and some of the girls try to hold him back. On the other side of frame, seated at the table, is the* THIEF.

VOICES: Out of here . . . get him out . . . grab him.

82

Ricci *pointing*: I want to talk to him.

Thief *rising slowly*: To me? . . . and who are you? I don't know you.

A Blonde *getting to her feet*: What a racket . . . Throw him out . . . I've got a headache.

Ricci *menacing in the din*: I want to talk to you.

Thief: Me?

A Brunette, *her arms around the* Thief: No, no . . .

Thief: I'm not scared. *To brunette.* Shut up. *To* Ricci. You want me?

Ricci: Yes.

Thief *walking away*: Well, here I am.

> *The uproar continues.* Ricci *jumps towards camera in medium close-up.*
>
> *He grabs the* Thief *by the collar and holds him tight.* (*Still on page 79*)

Thief: Let go . . . Let me go.

Ricci *in close-up*: Now I've got you . . . I want my bike.

Thief: Hey . . . stop . . . let me go . . . Are you going to let me go?

> *Camera tracks with* Ricci *who is pulling the* Thief *towards the door. Everyone is talking at once. A group of women push the two men into the reception room.*

Ricci: Come outside.

> Ricci *lets the* Thief *go, but stays next to him. The* Licensee *takes* Ricci *by the arm.* Ricci *takes the* Thief *by the arm. She pulls them to the front door, which she opens.*

Woman: This is just too much . . . in the best House in Rome . . . What will the commissioner say if he hears . . . ?

> Ricci *pulls the* Thief *out the door, and is in turn pushed out by the* Woman.

Licensee: That's enough . . . go out in the street to do your fighting.

> *The door closes violently behind* Ricci *and the* Thief. *Long shot of the street.* Bruno, *in the foreground, back*

to camera, is watching the arched portico, hopefully. His father appears with the THIEF, *whom he pushes brutally against the wall.*

THIEF : So what do you want . . .?

BRUNO *runs up to his father. In medium close-up,* RICCI *grabs the* THIEF *and pushes him ahead. He walks, frightened, before* RICCI *and* BRUNO, *who are not letting him out of reach.*

RICCI : I want what you took from me.

They continue walking, back to camera.

THIEF : Look . . . what did I take?

RICCI *furiously grabs the* THIEF *and pins him against the wall. Medium close-up of the two.*

RICCI *almost crying with rage* : My bicycle . . . you hear . . . my bicycle.

THIEF *trying to get away* : What bicycle? I'm no thief.

RICCI *stopping his escape* : Oh, no, you don't . . .

THIEF : Be careful . . . stop pushing me about . . . if you don't, I'll batter you into that wall.

RICCI : You'd better remember, quick! I'm not moving until you do.

THIEF : Listen to this bloke . . . he's crazy . . . out of his head.

RICCI *screaming* : It's you . . . you!

THIEF *held by the collar and worried* : Let me go . . . Let me go. I've had enough!

While they argue, a long shot of the street shows their shouts have attracted a crowd of people, who are approaching in silence. A man carrying a baby hears the dispute and turns back in the direction he came from.

RICCI *off* : I've had enough too!

THIEF *off* : Let me bloody well be! Let go.

RICCI : I'm not letting you go until you give me back the bike you stole in Fiorola yesterday.

Shot of BRUNO *worried by the gathering crowd.*

THIEF : I wasn't anywhere near Fiorola yesterday . . .

Medium close-up, shot slightly from above of the two men, surrounded by the crowd. (Still on page 79)

RICCI *shaking him* : Yes, you were . . . You were . . And you were wearing that cap.

RICCI *waves the* THIEF'S *cap in the air.*

BYSTANDER : Yes . . . well?

ANOTHER : So what does that prove? You just can't go around accusing people like that, you know.

Despite the hostility of the crowd, RICCI, *sure of his rights, continues to shake the* THIEF.

RICCI : You stay here . . . you understand. Now I've got you I'm not letting you go.

MOTHER *off* : Hey . . . you over there . . . What do you want with my boy?

Everyone looks up. Leaning out of an upstairs window is a white-haired woman. She is very angry.

MOTHER : Alfredo, get into the house this instant.

In the centre of the crowd, the THIEF *tries once again to break away, but* RICCI *once again grabs him.*

RICCI : No, you bastard . . . you're staying here.

THIEF *trembling* : Let me go . . . Don't touch me.

He seems to be on the brink of a fit. Two well-dressed but shifty-looking men push their way through the crowd. One with dark glasses, very sure of himself, approaches RICCI.

MAN IN DARK GLASSES : So someone pinched your bike, did they?

RICCI : Yes, my bike was stolen.

OTHER MAN : Before you go and accuse someone, are you sure it was him?

RICCI : Of course, I'm sure.

BYSTANDER : Where was it stolen?

RICCI : Near Fiorola.

OTHER MAN : If you're so sure, go and get a policeman. He's not going anywhere. He lives just here.

BRUNO, *at the mention of the police, starts to worm his*

85

way out of the crowd.

THIEF: Yes . . . go on. I'll be here. I've nothing to hide.

RICCI *grabs him.*

RICCI: No, you can't go. I'm not a fool. Stay where you are.

THIEF *becoming hysterical*: I never saw you before . . . Don't touch me.

MOTHER *off*: Oh, Alfredo . . . my poor little Alfredo.

His cap falls to the ground and he begins to shake uncontrollably. RICCI, anxious but sceptical, lets him go. Held up by some of the bystanders, he does not fall straight down, but instead sinks slowly to the ground in the grip of a fit. He foams at the mouth. Long shot of RICCI, dumbfounded. The MAN IN DARK GLASSES taps him on the shoulder.

MAN IN DARK GLASSES: I think you'd better get out of here.

VOICES *off*: Be careful with him . . . Hold his arm.

OTHER MAN: See what you've done . . . you happy now?

MAN IN DARK GLASSES: You can't accuse people like that . . .

MOTHER *moaning*: Oh, oh . . . Alfredo . . . Be careful of his head . . . his head.

Medium close-up of RICCI lowering his head. Pan down with his gaze onto the THIEF in the midst of a real epileptic attack with the crowd around him.

MAN IN DARK GLASSES *to* RICCI: I wouldn't stay here if I were you.

Medium shot of the MOTHER with a pillow for her son's head.

MOTHER: Alfredo . . . Alfredo . . . what does he want, that man? Make him go away . . . Oh, my boy, my boy . . . Put this under his head . . . Holy Mother . . .

Pan with her as she kneels down next to her son.

MOTHER: There . . . there . . . my little one . . .

Medium close-up of RICCI, surrounded by an angry crowd, pushing and threatening him.

BYSTANDERS: You still here . . . We told you to disappear

. . . Go on, get out of here . . . We don't want to see your ugly face any more!

RICCI *enraged*: Get your hands off me . . . you're all thieves . . . *Screaming now* . . . All . . . all of you!

BYSTANDERS *forcing* RICCI *back*: Watch your tongue . . . you should be careful about name calling . . . remember where you are . . . you could lose more than a bicycle . . .

They have RICCI *backed up against a wall, their expressions and gestures becoming more and more menacing. Finally,* RICCI *picks up a long piece of wood which he waves defiantly. (Still on page 80)*

RICCI: Leave me alone . . . it's a hundred against one, you thugs . . . I'll smash in all your faces . . .

BYSTANDERS: Just try — go on, just try . . . you sure you're not round the bend . . . look, he's barmy . . .

RICCI: You bastards . . . thieves, thieves, thieves!

High angle long shot of the crowd, encircling RICCI. *The contents of a bucket of water falls on them, and they look up.*

BYSTANDERS: Hey, what's the matter with you . . . what do you think you're doing?

Pan up to a man in shirt-sleeves holding the empty pail.

MAN: I was just trying to cool the fellow down a bit . . .

They all laugh. Long shot of the street: in the distance BRUNO *appears with a* POLICEMAN. BRUNO *points to the crowd. Medium shot of* RICCI *still holding his weapon ready. When he sees the* POLICEMAN, *he drops it. The crowd discreetly moves away from* RICCI. *Medium shot of the* POLICEMAN *passing in front of the* MOTHER *who is still holding her son's head.*

POLICEMAN: Well, where's the owner of this bicycle?

RICCI *in medium close-up comes forward*: Here I am . . . That's him . . . *Pointing to the* THIEF . . . putting on his act.

Medium close-up of some of the men in the crowd.

BYSTANDER: What do you mean 'an act'?

ANOTHER: If he was acting you'd know it.

87

ANOTHER: **He's really ill.**

ANOTHER: Poor bloke . . . when someone accuses you like that there's good reason to get sick . . . he's had a breakdown . . .

THIEF *raising his head with an effort*: I'll explain everything, officer . . . innnn a little while . . . I . . . I've nothing to hide.

MOTHER: What's he got against my boy? He's honest . . . Everyone here knows that.

ANOTHER: Poor Alfredo . . . I've never seen him in such a state.

MOTHER: Everyone will stand up for him. He's a good boy.

EVERYONE: Yes . . . he is.

ANOTHER: He says it's because of his German cap.

ANOTHER *waving his cap*: And this . . . what's this . . . ? It's not German.

Laughter.

POLICEMAN *to the* THIEF: Come on . . . get up.

MOTHER: But he can't even move!

ANOTHER: He'd be better off in a hospital . . .

POLICEMAN *to* MOTHER: Well, then, show us into the house. Come on.

A pan, then camera tracks forward with the MOTHER *as she leads the way.*

MOTHER: You're very welcome. It's the home of good honest people . . . You'll see . . . This way.

She enters the building first, followed by the POLICEMAN, *then* RICCI *and* BRUNO. *A man and a woman are leaning against the wall on either side of the door.*

MAN *looking at* RICCI: I'd have him up in court.

WOMAN *harshly to* RICCI: What do you want from Alfredo? He wouldn't hurt a fly.

The narrow stairway leading to the THIEF'S *home.*

The door opens and the group, led by the MOTHER, *go into the apartment. She moves around the single room, which is not very large, dirty, and bare. The others stand between the door now closed, and a stove with a large pot on it. Pan with the* MOTHER.

MOTHER: Here we are . . . There's not much to see. There are four of us. Him . . . he sleeps here . . . *Lifting up the mattress* . . . You can look under the bed for the bike if you wish! . . . *Continuing her tour of the room* . . . There's my daughter's bed and there, the other boy. This one's mine . . .

She lifts up the lid of the pot on the stove and turns towards the others who are out of shot.

MOTHER: Instead of coming here to accuse him, you'd do better to find him a job. The poor boy, he's been looking for such a long time. Poor soul.

The end of her remark is spoken off. The POLICEMAN *and* RICCI *find an automobile tyre hidden under some washing. The* MOTHER *is unnerved but trying to hide it.*

MOTHER: Oh that . . . belonged to my brother-in-law . . . for an 1100 he had . . . he asked me to keep them here for a while. Go on, search everywhere . . . See if you can find any bicycles.

Medium shot of the POLICEMAN *looking more or less everywhere.* RICCI *and* BRUNO *conduct their own investigation. Cut to the* MOTHER *watching them. Pan with the* POLICEMAN *as he walks to the corner of the room and makes a sign to* RICCI.

POLICEMAN *wispering*: Listen . . . do you have a witness?

RICCI: I am a witness.

Close-up of the MOTHER *who is trying to make out their conversation. The* POLICEMAN *turns to her.*

POLICEMAN *pointing to the door*: Would you mind going out for a moment?

Pan with her as she walks to the door.

MOTHER *muttering*: You can talk for an hour . . . two hours . . . it makes no difference to me!

She slams the door behind her. Medium close-up of the POLICEMAN *and* RICCI, *seen from below, from* BRUNO'S *point of view. They move towards the window.*

POLICEMAN: By yourself . . . you could be mistaken . . . Are

89

you sure you recognized him?

RICCI : Yes . . . Of course, I did.

POLICEMAN *now next to the window* : Come here.

Low angle from the street of the two looking out the window. High angle of the street from the window. Some men are standing around the THIEF. *They turn and look up at the window.*

POLICEMAN : Look down there . . . All those people are witnesses for him.

Interior of the room. The two men walk towards BRUNO.

POLICEMAN : I see things like this every day. You're wasting your time . . . Did you see him full face?

RICCI : Yes, I saw him as he was getting away.

POLICEMAN : From the back . . .

RICCI : No . . . I had time to see him because . . . I really saw him.

The POLICEMAN, *rather sceptical, takes a few steps and stops by the window.* RICCI *faces him. In the foreground,* BRUNO *looks up at them. In the background, a woman carrying a baby closes the window in the building across the street. (Still on page 80)*

POLICEMAN : Tell me . . . were there many people there?

RICCI : Yes, there were.

POLICEMAN : And you couldn't find anyone to be a witness?

RICCI : I had other things to do besides taking names.

They walk towards the door. The POLICEMAN *signals to the* MOTHER *to come back in, which she does. Just as they are about to go out, a shoddily-dressed young girl comes in, carrying some packages, and gives* RICCI *a nasty look. She puts her packages down on the table in the foreground. In the background, the door shuts behind* RICCI, BRUNO, *and the* POLICEMAN.

Low angle of the stairway, the POLICEMAN *leading the way. He stops and turns to* RICCI *and* BRUNO.

POLICEMAN : In summary . . . you never saw his face . . . you have no witnesses . . . You may be right, but you have no proof. And if he was found innocent, you'd be in trouble. You either have to catch him in the act or find the bicycle in his possession . . . Without that, nothing can be done.

RICCI: Yes . . . Well . . . I'll smash his face in.

POLICEMAN *going downstairs*: If you do, I'll have to put you inside.

RICCI *motionless and murmuring*: If you only knew what this business means to me!

Cut to mid-shot of the POLICEMAN *near the street door.*

POLICEMAN *to the* THIEF: Hey . . . come here.

The THIEF *and some of his friends come over to them. The* POLICEMAN *takes out his notebook.* RICCI *is half-hidden behind him.*

OTHER MAN *to* RICCI: You happy now? What did you find? Nothing . . . of course. Go on, get out of here.

THIEF *to* POLICEMAN: I'm innocent . . . Believe me, I'm innocent.

POLICEMAN: What's your name?

THIEF: Alfredo Catelli. I live here. I feel better now, I'll come with you.

POLICEMAN *taking notes, to* RICCI: Do you want to charge him?

MOTHER *from the door*: He's innocent . . . you hear, innocent . . .

RICCI, holding BRUNO *by the hand, abruptly pushes his way through the crowd and moves away. Camera stays on the crowd.*

VOICES: Too bad . . . Get away from here . . . quick . . . don't come back here again if you know what's good for you . . . accusing people like that.

MAN IN DARK GLASSES: Piss off . . . We've seen enough of you.

RICCI, pushing his way by some people at the end of the street. He has, in his fury, let go of BRUNO. RICCI, *back to camera, walks alone. Camera tracks in on him.*

VOICES *merging into one voice, partly off*: What's your name?

91

Don't forget Via Panico. Coward. Liar. Cuckold. Big head. You wouldn't get away with accusing me.

RICCI *stops suddenly at the corner and turns back. Fast track in on him. Cut to the suddenly silent crowd.* RICCI *turns back and walks down an empty street. Walking towards camera, he stops, realising that he is alone. He runs back to the corner.*

RICCI : Bruno . . . Come on . . . !

Long shot of the empty street. BRUNO *joins his father and follows a few paces behind him. The crowd moves after them for a bit, still shouting.*

Father and son walk down various streets. Dissolve. RICCI *walks like an automaton, his fists clenched.* BRUNO, *worried about his father, looks up at him from time to time.*

Long shot of a large piazza. BRUNO *is having difficulty in keeping up. They cross the piazza.* BRUNO *nearly gets hit by a passing car, but* RICCI *does not even notice. Another car slams on its brakes to avoid* BRUNO. *They go down a long flight of steps. Dissolve. They are walking towards the municipal stadium. Medium shot of* RICCI *and* BRUNO *as they arrive near a bus stop.* RICCI *stops, and* BRUNO *sits down on the kerb to get his breath back. Medium close-up of* RICCI, *his eyes shining, looking out of shot. Cut to a general shot of rows and rows of bicycles parked outside the stadium. The roar of the football crowd in the stadium can be heard over.* RICCI *looks down at* BRUNO *who is scratching his head.* RICCI, *hands firmly in his pockets, walks up and down nervously. He looks towards the bikes near the stadium, then walks away and looks down a small street. Long shot of the sunny street, near the door of a building, where an old bicycle leans, unguarded, against the wall. Close-up of* RICCI *who considers for a second then turns away. Pan in mid-shot as* RICCI *goes and sits on the kerb next to* BRUNO. (Still on page 97) *His son looks at him, surprised.*

RICCI, *exhausted, lowers his head. He stays immobile and silent, then with a roar from the crowd, he looks up. Cut to long shot of the stadium. Cut back to father and son.* RICCI *rubs his eyes and face nervously with his hand. In the foreground a group of racing cyclists ride by.* RICCI *seems provoked into action by them. After they have passed,* RICCI *gets quickly to his feet. He looks towards the stadium. Cut to the stadium in long shot. Quick intercut shots of* RICCI, *the parked bicycles; back to* RICCI; *some people walking across the piazza next to the stadium; shot of* RICCI *and the piazza in long shot.* RICCI *turns away and walks towards the adjacent street to make sure that the bicycle is still there. He leans against the wall. Cut to* BRUNO, *still seated, who has been watching his father's curious movements. (Still on page 98) Medium close-up of* RICCI *sweating, as he turns and looks once again towards the stadium parking area. Long shot of the rows of bikes and the stadium. Its gates have opened, and the people are coming out of the stadium. Some young people are riding off on their bicycles. Track with* RICCI *as he paces. After taking his hat off and running his hand contemplatively through his hair, he walks up to* BRUNO, *knowing what course of action he is going to take. He takes some coins from his pocket and gives them to* BRUNO.

RICCI: Here, Bruno . . . take that tram to Monte Sacro and wait for me.

BRUNO *puzzled*: Where?

RICCI *pushing*: Come on . . . Do as you're told . . . Run . . . there's the tram.

BRUNO *crosses the street. Track in with* RICCI *as he moves across the street where the bicycle is against the wall.*
BRUNO *trots off towards the waiting tram. The bell rings and the doors close before* BRUNO *gets on. He stands and watches the tram move away.*
Long shot of the street. RICCI *walks, outwardly calm,*

towards camera. He gives the bike a cursory glance in passing. (Still on page 99) He stops about twenty feet past the bike, turns, runs, and jumps on the bike, which he pedals furiously. A man comes shooting out of the door by which the bike was standing.

OWNER *shouting*: Thief . . . Thief . . . Stop him . . . Thief . . . Stop him!

Long shot of the street. RICCI, *riding as fast as he can, turns into the next street. Called to attention by the* OWNER'S *shout, some men take up the chase. In long shot, slightly from above,* RICCI *is losing ground as he rides across a piazza. A tram passes.*

PURSUERS: Thief . . . Thief . . . Get him!

Cut to another street, RICCI *still losing ground to the agile young men. (Still on page 99) People shouting.*

PURSUERS: Run . . . Run . . . We'll catch him . . . Thief . . .

Medium shot of BRUNO *who, on hearing the cries, turns to see his father's ignoble race. He is surprised, alarmed, and very unhappy.*

Long shot of RICCI *pedalling in the direction of the stadium. One of the men reaches out and grabs* RICCI'S *coat. He loses his balance, and falls to the ground, the bike on top of him. The crowd rushes to surround him. Medium close-up of* BRUNO, *horrified, as he runs to his father. General shot of the crowd gathered around* RICCI. *He is on his feet, defending himself against the blows and the insults.*

VOICES: Thief . . . Swine . . . Criminal.

The OWNER, *dragging the bicycle along, reaches the edge of the crowd. He drops the bike and pushes his way to the centre of the fight. Medium close-up of* RICCI *held by three men and the* OWNER. *The crowd gets bigger around them.*

OWNER *angry and out of breath*: Bastard . . . I'll teach you to rob people.

MEN: Teach him a lesson . . . Give it to him . . . *One of the men pushes him . . .* Thief!

OWNER: You faceless scoundrel . . .

MEN: Take care of him . . . Yes . . . Prison . . . That'll show him . . . the bugger.

As they hit him, his hat falls to the ground. Medium close-up of BRUNO *trying to reach his father.*

BRUNO: Papa . . . papa . . .

Medium close-up of RICCI *surrounded by glaring faces. Everyone is shouting at once.* RICCI *looks completely destroyed. He is not even trying to protect himself.*

High angle long shot, as the crowd moves aside to let a tram pass. Two men push RICCI *forward.* BRUNO *stands alone near the tram rails. Now* RICCI *is caught and in custody most of the crowd have resumed their strolling.* BRUNO *picks up* RICCI'S *hat, dusts it off, and walks towards camera with tears running down his cheeks. Track with* RICCI *and his two guards across the parking lot. Behind them a handful of other men as well as the* OWNER. (*Still on page 100*)

MAN: Where do we take him?

OWNER: There's a police station over there.

MAN *off*: Not all of us should go. Just a couple of witnesses and the owner . . . that's all.

They stop walking as BRUNO *runs up and grabs his father's legs.* (*Still on page 100*) *He glares at them in rage. Medium close-up of* RICCI *looking down at his son. Pan down with his look to* BRUNO *looking up at his father. The* OWNER *watches both father and son. He seems fed-up and deflated.*

OWNER: Come on . . . I don't want to make trouble . . . not for anyone. *Off, close-up of* RICCI. Let's just forget it.

MAN *off*: You ought to put him behind bars.

OWNER: Let him go . . . Good-bye and thank you all.

He moves out of shot. BRUNO *is drying his eyes.*

MAN *off*: That's a nice trick to teach your son.

Medium shot of the small group of men.

MAN: You're lucky you didn't have to deal with me. I'd have shown you a thing or two. Clear off . . . Go on . . . Get home.

He pushes RICCI, *as does another man.*

ANOTHER: You can thank the Lord you got out of that . . . you crook!

Camera tracks with RICCI *and* BRUNO *as they walk slowly across the parking area. The sound of indistinct insults follows them. People walk by, as they do on any Sunday afternoon.* BRUNO *discreetly hands his father the hat.* RICCI *takes it and straightens his hair. Track back in medium close-up of* RICCI *walking, his jaw set, eyes empty of emotion, shoulders sagging. Medium close-up of* BRUNO *hugging his father's legs, and still wiping the odd tear from his face. They move through the lolling crowd. The lorry full of Modena supporters passes. Shots of* BRUNO *and* RICCI *walking.*

Track back in medium close-up to RICCI, *still looking lost; walking with whatever force he can muster. Pan down to* BRUNO *looking up to his father. He is unhappy about what has happened and miserable because he can do nothing about it. Pan back up to* RICCI *who has lowered his head. His lips are trembling.* RICCI *tries to hold back the tears in his eyes. He continues to walk with a faltering step. Close-up of* BRUNO *walking next to his father still looking up at him. Big close-up of* BRUNO'S *hand slipping into his father's.* RICCI *squeezes the hand as if he cannot make up his mind whether he wants to kiss it or crush it. Shot of* RICCI *walking on and crying;* BRUNO *holding his father's hand. Big close-up of their hands. Long shot from behind them, as they move away and disappear into the gathering crowd.* 'THE END' *comes up over the final shot.*

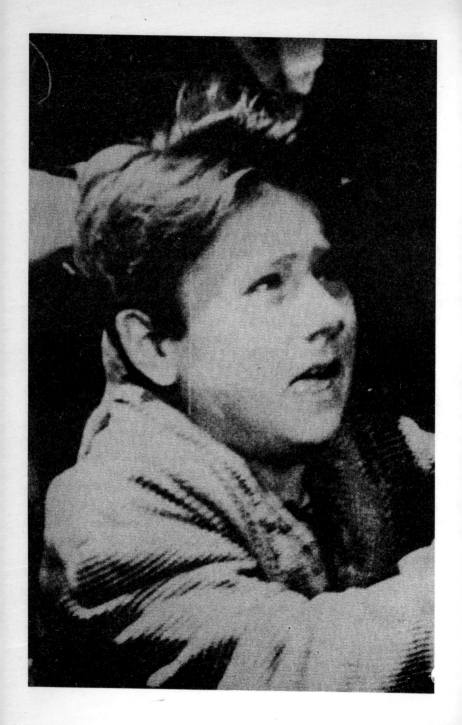